PLAY THE BLUES LIKE...

Learn to play in open tunings through the work of 12 blues greats, with standard notation and tablature, along with historical information

By Pete Madsen

string
letter
media

Publisher: David A. Lusterman
Editor: Adam Perlmutter
Managing Editor: Kevin Owens
Design and Production: Bill Evans
Production Manager: Hugh O'Connor

Cover Illustration: Olivia Wise

ISBN 978-1-936604-28-9

Printed in the United States of America
All rights reserved.
This book was produced by Stringletter Media, Inc.
501 Canal Blvd., Suite J, Richmond, CA 94804
(510) 215-0010; stringletter.com

Names: Madsen, Pete, author.
Title: Play the blues like... : learn to play in open tunings through the
  work of 12 blues greats, with standard notation and tablature, along with
  historical information / by Pete Madsen.
Description: Richmond, CA : String Letter Publishing, 2018. | Series:
  Acoustic guitar. Private lessons
Identifiers: LCCN 2018032302 | ISBN 9781936604289 (51999 : alk. paper)
Subjects: LCSH: Guitar--Methods (Blues)--Self-instruction. | Guitar music
  (Blues)--Instruction and study.
Classification: LCC MT588 .M19 2018 | DDC 787.87/1931643--dc23
LC record available at https://lccn.loc.gov/2018032302

Contents

Video downloads to accompany each of the lessons and musical examples in *Scottish Songs for Guitar* are available for free at **store.acousticguitar.com/PTBLvideo**. Just add the video tracks to your shopping cart and check out to get your free download.

Introduction

Welcome to *Play the Blues Like....* If you are a student of blues guitar, you have probably at some point been intrigued by exploring alternate tunings with a bottleneck slide. Open tunings provide a world of possibilities—and limitations. Your normal fingerings for chords and scales are thrown out the window, forcing you to view the fretboard in new ways.

Luckily, the blues is fairly straightforward: three chords, 12 bars, and off you go. This framework keeps the task manageable. For instance, if you're playing in open-G tuning, you really only need to know the locations of the I, IV, and V chords (G, C, and D). If you want to expand your knowledge of the fretboard in a given tuning, you can use what you learned from studying blues as a starting point.

While the players represented in this book use similar tunings and chord structures, I am often struck by their unique sounds and phrasing. Booker White's playing in open D minor is very different from Skip James' playing in the same tuning; Memphis Minnie in open G is clearly distinct from Son House in open G.

Each lesson in this guide demonstrates key licks and phrases of a particular artist and ends with a short new piece that places everything in a typical blues context, like the 12-bar form. There is a lesson here: blues, like folk music, is all about making it your own. The ultimate goal is to study the greats and piece together what you have learned in a unique way. The more sources you borrow from, the less you sound like, say, a Robert Johnson clone, and the more you sound like a player who is steeped in the blues.

This book is not meant to be a definitive tome on blues guitarists who play in open tunings. It is, however, a diverse collection of some of the very best. Some are household names (Robert Johnson, Jimmy Page); others are less well-known (R. L. Burnside, Memphis Minnie), but their contributions to the genre should not be underestimated.

Some players emphasized groove (Burnside, Alvin Youngblood Hart), while others focused on mood (Jimmy Page, Skip James) and precise technique (Tampa Red). Two of these fingerpickers (Memphis Minnie and Elizabeth Cotten) are known for defying gender norms by playing guitar. And all of these great musicians contributed to the overall spectrum of what we call blues.

One of the most prevalent tunings in blues is Spanish, or open-G tuning (low to high: D G D G B D, sometimes played as open A: E A E A C# E). You'll see a lot of open G in this book. The commonness of this tuning is likely related to the popularity of the banjo—usually tuned to some version of open G—in late-19th and early-20th-century America. Banjo was not always a great match for the human voice, and so players gravitated towards the guitar, appropriating banjo tunings and fingerstyle technique.

Another popular blues tuning is Vestapol, or open D (D A D F# A D)/open E (E B E G# B E). In this book, you'll work with open D, which is a great tuning for creating a heavy sound with alternating-bass patterns on the open sixth and fourth strings. The name Vestapol comes from "The Battle of Sevastapol," a mid-19th century parlor song. It's unclear how a Crimean war song became popular with blues musicians, but many players, including Elizabeth Cotten, had a version of it. You'll also work in another variant of Vestapol, open D minor (D A D F A D).

Unlike a traditional method book, which builds upon itself chapter by chapter in linear fashion, this guide is perfect for skipping around. Of course, some players' techniques are harder than others to master. I find Kelly Joe Phelps' approach particularly challenging. Work through as many of these lessons as possible, so that you can gain an understanding of the possibilities inherent to each tuning while acquiring a rich blues vocabulary to draw from. Enjoy the journey!

—*Pete Madsen*

Notation Guide

Reading music is no different than reading a book. In both cases, you need to understand the language that you're reading; you can't read Chinese characters if you don't understand them, and you can't read music if you don't understand the written symbols behind music notation.

Guitarists use several types of notation, including standard notation, tablature, and chord grids. Standard notation is the main notation system common to all instruments and styles in Western music. Knowing standard notation will allow you to share and play music with almost any other instrument. Tablature is a notation system exclusively for stringed instruments with frets—like guitar and mandolin—that shows you what strings and frets to play at any given moment. Chord grids use a graphic representation of the fretboard to show chord shapes for fretted stringed instruments. Here's a primer on how to read these types of notation.

Standard Notation

Standard notation is written on a five-line staff. Notes are written in alphabetical order from A to G. Every time you pass a G note, the sequence of notes repeats—starting with A.

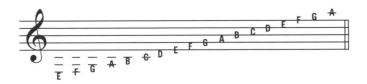

The duration of a note is determined by three things: the note head, stem, and flag. A whole note (o) equals four beats. A half note (𝅗𝅥) is half of that: two beats. A quarter note (♩) equals one beat, an eighth note (♪) equals half of one beat, and a 16th note (♬) is a quarter beat (there are four 16th notes per beat).

The fraction (4/4, 3/4, 6/8, etc.) or ¢ character shown at the beginning of a piece of music denotes the time signature. The top number tells you how many beats are in each measure, and the bottom number indicates the rhythmic value of each beat (4 equals a quarter note, 8 equals an eighth note, 16 equals a 16th note, and 2 equals a half note).

The most common time signature is 4/4, which signifies four quarter notes per measure and is sometimes designated with the symbol ¢ (for common time). The symbol ¢ stands for cut time (2/2). Most songs are either in 4/4 or 3/4.

Tablature

In tablature, the six horizontal lines represent the six strings of the guitar, with the first string on the top and sixth on the bottom. The numbers refer to fret numbers on a given string.

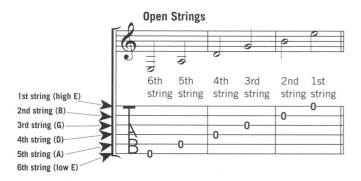

The notation and tablature in this book are designed to be used in tandem—refer to the notation to get the rhythmic information and note durations, and refer to the tablature to get the exact locations of the notes on the guitar fingerboard.

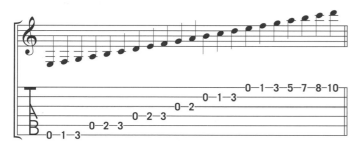

Fingerings

Fingerings are indicated with small numbers and letters in the notation. Fretting-hand fingering is indicated with 1 for the index finger, 2 the middle, 3 the ring, 4 the pinky, and *T* the thumb. Picking-hand fingering is indicated by *i* for the index finger, *m* the middle, *a* the ring, *c* the pinky, and *p* the thumb. Circled numbers indicate the string the note is played on. Remember that the fingerings indicated are only suggestions; if you find a different way that works better for you, use it.

Strumming and Picking

In music played with a flatpick, downstrokes (toward the floor) and upstrokes (toward the ceiling) are shown as follows. Slashes in the notation and tablature indicate a strum through the previously played chord.

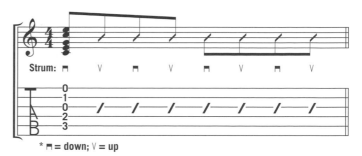

In music played with the pick-hand fingers, *split stems* are often used to highlight the division between thumb and fingers. With split stems, notes played by the thumb have stems pointing down, while notes played by the fingers have stems pointing up. If split stems are not used, pick-hand fingerings are usually present. Here is the same fingerpicking pattern shown with and without split stems.

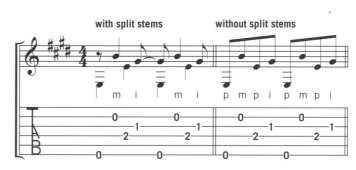

Chord Diagrams

Chord diagrams show where the fingers go on the fingerboard. Frets are shown horizontally. The thick top line represents the nut. A fret number to the right of a diagram indicates a chord played higher up the neck (in this case the top horizontal line is thin). Strings are shown as vertical lines. The line on the far left represents the sixth (lowest) string, and the line on the far right represents the first (highest) string. Dots show where the fingers go, and thick horizontal lines indicate barres. Numbers above the diagram are left-hand finger numbers, as used in standard notation.

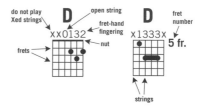

Again, the fingerings are only suggestions. An *X* indicates a string that should be muted or not played; 0 indicates an open string.

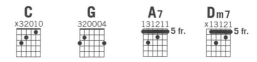

Capos

If a capo is used, a Roman numeral indicates the fret where the capo should be placed. The standard notation and tablature is written as if the capo were the nut of the guitar. For instance, a tune capoed anywhere up the neck and played using key-of-G chord shapes and fingerings will be written in the key of G. Likewise, open strings held down by the capo are written as open strings.

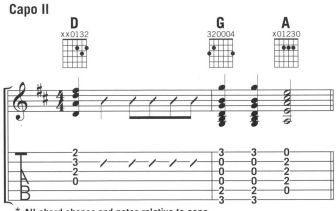

* All chord shapes and notes relative to capo

Tunings

Alternate guitar tunings are given from the lowest (sixth) string to the highest (first) string. For instance, D A D G B E indicates standard tuning with the bottom string dropped to D. Standard notation for songs in alternate tunings always reflects the actual pitches of the notes. Arrows underneath tuning notes indicate strings that are altered from standard tuning and whether they are tuned up or down.

Tuning: D A D G B E

Vocal Tunes

Vocal tunes are sometimes written with a fully tabbed-out introduction and a vocal melody with chord diagrams for the rest of the piece. The tab intro is usually your indication of which strum or fingerpicking pattern to use in the rest of the piece. The melody with lyrics underneath is the melody sung by the vocalist. Occasionally, smaller notes are written with the melody to indicate other instruments or the harmony part sung by another vocalist. These are not to be confused with cue notes, which are small notes that indicate melodies that vary when a section is repeated. Listen to a recording of the piece to get a feel for the guitar accompaniment and to hear the singing if you aren't skilled at reading vocal melodies.

Articulations

There are a number of ways you can articulate a note on the guitar. Notes connected with slurs (not to be confused with ties) in the tablature or standard notation are articulated with either a hammer-on, pull-off, or slide. Lower notes slurred to higher notes are played as hammer-ons; higher notes slurred to lower notes are played as pull-offs.

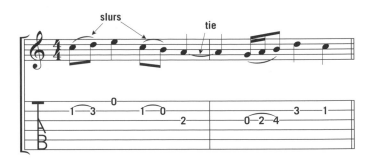

Slides are represented with a dash, and an S is included above the tab. A dash preceding a note represents a slide into the note from an indefinite point in the direction of the slide; a dash following a note indicates a slide off of the note to an indefinite point in the direction of the slide. For two slurred notes connected with a slide, you should pick the first note and then slide into the second.

Bends are represented with upward curves, as shown in the next example. Most bends have a specific destination pitch—the number above the bend symbol shows how much the bend raises the string's pitch: ¼ for a slight bend, ½ for a half step, 1 for a whole step.

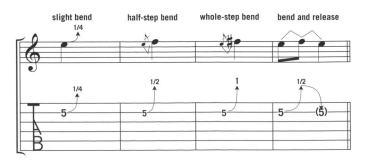

Grace notes are represented by small notes with a dash through the stem in standard notation and with small numbers in the tab. A grace note is a very quick ornament leading into a note, most commonly executed as a hammer-on, pull-off, or slide. In the first example below, pluck the note at the fifth fret on the beat, then quickly hammer onto the seventh fret. The second example is executed as a quick pull-off from the second fret to the open string. In the third example, both notes at the fifth fret are played simultaneously (even though it appears that the fifth fret, fourth string, is to be played by itself), then the seventh fret, fourth string, is quickly hammered.

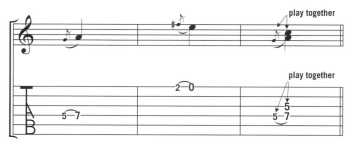

Harmonics

Harmonics are represented by diamond-shaped notes in the standard notation and a small dot next to the tablature numbers. Natural harmonics are indicated with the text "Harmonics" or "Harm." above the tablature. Harmonics articulated with the right hand (often called artificial harmonics) include the text "R.H. Harmonics" or "R.H. Harm." above the tab. Right-hand harmonics are executed by lightly touching the harmonic node (usually 12 frets above the open string or fretted note) with the right-hand index finger and plucking the string with the thumb or ring finger or pick. For extended phrases played with right-hand harmonics, the fretted notes are shown in the tab along with instructions to touch the harmonics 12 frets above the notes.

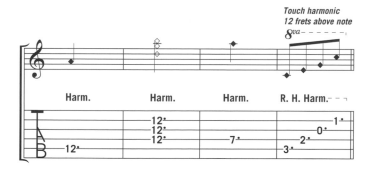

Repeats

One of the most confusing parts of a musical score can be the navigation symbols, such as repeats, *D.S. al Coda*, *D.C. al Fine*, *To Coda*, etc. Repeat symbols are placed at the beginning and end of the passage to be repeated.

You should ignore repeat symbols with the dots on the right side the first time you encounter them; when you come to a repeat symbol with dots on the left side, jump back to the previous repeat symbol facing the opposite direction (if there is no previous symbol, go to the beginning of the piece). The next time you come to the repeat symbol, ignore it and keep going unless it includes instructions such as "Repeat three times."

A section will often have a different ending after each repeat. The example below includes a first and a second ending. Play until you hit the repeat symbol, jump back to the previous repeat symbol and play until you reach the bracketed first ending, skip the measures under the bracket and jump immediately to the second ending, and then continue.

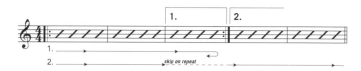

D.S. stands for *dal segno* or "from the sign." When you encounter this indication, jump immediately to the sign (𝄋). *D.S.* is usually accompanied by *al Fine* or *al Coda*. Fine indicates the end of a piece. A coda is a final passage near the end of a piece and is indicated with ⊕. *D.S. al Coda* simply tells you to jump back to the sign and continue on until you are instructed to jump to the coda, indicated with *To Coda* ⊕.

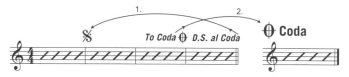

D.C. stands for *da capo* or "from the beginning." Jump to the top of the piece when you encounter this indication.

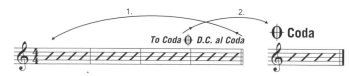

D.C. al Fine tells you to jump to the beginning of a tune and continue until you encounter the *Fine* indicating the end of the piece (ignore the *Fine* the first time through).

Getting Started

On the surface blues is fairly simplistic: three chords, 12 bars—and some attitude. But, as the saying goes, "It's not what you play, but how you play it." As you study the players represented in this guide, you will find that they mainly stick to the same sonic palette, but that the phrases have an individual personality that registers as each player's trademark sound. Before you dive into these players' styles, however, it might be useful to get familiar with the tools these artists are working with.

The Scales

Pentatonic scales provide a lot of meat for the blues, both in terms of melody and harmony. The minor pentatonic scale's formula is 1 ♭3 4 5 ♭7. **Example 1** shows a two-octave G minor pentatonic scale (G B♭ C D F) in open G tuning (low to high: D G D G B D). Of course, it would be useful to learn this scale all over the neck, but getting familiar with it in this position will go a long way toward understanding the music in this book.

The formula for the major pentatonic scale is 1 2 3 5 6. **Example 2** shows G major pentatonic (G A B D E). Though the minor pentatonic is the most common scale in blues and rock, many of the early blues players used the major version as often as the minor.

The Chords

Example 3 shows you one-finger versions of G and G7 chords in open G, and **Example 4** depicts a G7 chord played a bit higher up the neck. New chords can be formed by simply barring strings at any given fret. In some instances, you'll barre five strings, like in the C chord in **Example 5**, and other times just four strings, such as the C/G chord of that same example.

Another common chord voicing for C7 is shown in **Example 6**. This looks like a regular C chord, but with the altered tuning, the note at the third fret of string 5 is B♭, not C. The second version of this chord puts the open G in the bass with the B♭ played on the third string. Meanwhile, **Examples 7 and 8** are common voicings for D, D7, and D9 chords in open G.

Blues Fingerpicking

If you are not already familiar with monotonic or alternating bass patterns, you should find the next few exercises useful. In general, use your thumb to pick strings 6–4 and either use your index and middle fingers or index, middle, and ring fingers on the top three strings. The following abbreviations are used for the picking-hand fingers: p = thumb, i = index, m = middle, and a = ring.

In **Example 9**, pick a steady bass pattern with your thumb on string 5, adding double stops on strings 1 and 2 with your ring and middle (or middle and index) fingers. Make sure to tap your foot and play the bass notes squarely on the downbeats. **Example 10** uses the same bass pattern as in Ex. 9, but with single notes on the top three strings. Switch to an alternating bass for **Examples 11 and 12**, using your thumb to navigate between strings 5 and 4.

Bottleneck Slide Guitar

Playing in an open tuning is a good invitation to try some bottleneck slide. Many of the lessons in this guide will give you an opportunity to work on that aspect of your playing. Here are some tips for what kind of slide might best suit your needs. Buy a small assortment of slides to find which type works best for you.

Materials

Metal/brass, glass, or ceramic slides are generally preferable for bottleneck blues. Glass tends to be a little smoother-sounding than metal, but metal is generally louder. I like the sound of brass, but unless you keep it polished, it has a tendency to feel sticky. These days I prefer ceramic, which seems to combine the best qualities of metal and glass; it slides better on the string with a consistent pressure. Metal slides usually have thinner walls and are therefore a bit easier to direct place accurately, directly above the fret. The heavier the slide the more sound you get, so for acoustic guitar I recommend using a slide that has some mass. On the other hand, the heavier the slide, the harder it is to control.

Wearing a Slide

Many players place the slide on their fourth finger. This will give you the most flexibility, allowing your first, second, and third fingers to fret other strings and make chords. Other players—some presented in this book—place the slide on their third, middle, or even first finger. Whatever finger you choose, the slide should fit snuggly. You can compensate for a loose-fitting slide by stuffing it with foam or candlewax.

Keep in mind that you don't need to apply too much pressure to the string when playing slide. It's more important to keep consistent contact as you slide from note to note. The bottleneck should only cover as many strings as you're playing slide notes on. For instance, if you're playing a slide line on the first string, keep the bottleneck off of strings 2–5. Also, tilt the slide slightly away from the fretboard, to avoid hitting other strings and producing unwanted overtones.

In **Example 13**, climb up the neck on the first string with the slide. Pay careful attention to the quality of the sound as you move from note to note. For example, the first slide you play is from G to F; make sure you target the fretwire to achieve the proper intonation. Play up the neck to the 12th fret and then work your way back to the third fret.

Tuning: D G D G B D

Example 1

G minor pentatonic

Example 2

G major pentatonic

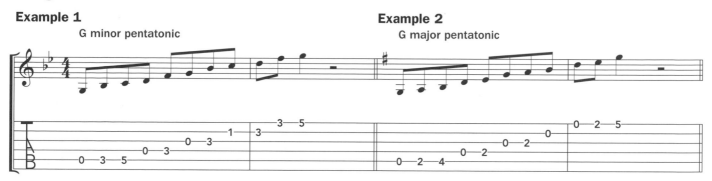

Examples 3–8

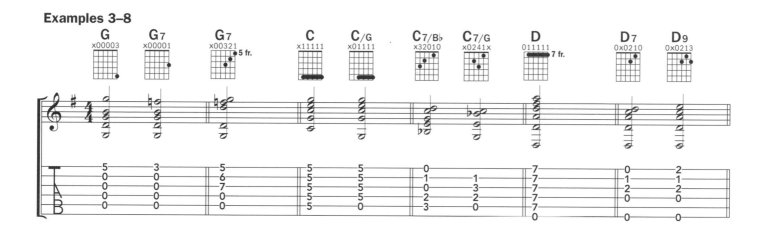

Example 9

G7

Example 10

G

Example 11

G

Example 12

G

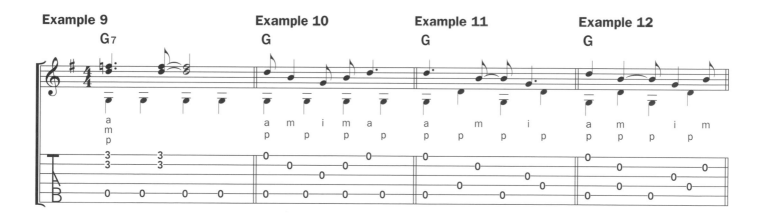

Example 13

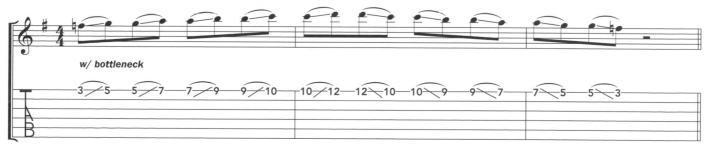

w/ bottleneck

String Damping

A critical aspect of slide playing is string damping, which can be achieved with both hands. This technique will cut down on unwanted transient noises. As you drag the slide across the strings, use one or more of your available fretting fingers to touch and drag along that string with the slide. I opt for my first finger, which results in my middle and ring fingers resting on top of the slide.

In **Example 14**, dip the bottleneck inwards to cover both the first and second strings. Slide up on the second string and then pick the first string. You can either keep the slide in contact with both strings or tilt the slide outwards, effectively cutting off the sound on the second string, as you play the first string.

Example 15 uses the third string (G) to create a short ascending lick in which every other note is open. Try to tilt the slide in and use your dampening finger to deaden the string between slide notes and before you pick the open string. You can also pull off from the bottleneck-produced notes to sound the open string.

Open-D Tuning

Just as you did with open G, explore some of the foundational aspects of open-D tuning. Start with **Examples 16** and **17**, the D minor and major pentatonic scales, respectively.

Examples 18–23 show you some of the common I, IV, and V shapes in open D. Obviously, the open strings played together (**Example 18**) outline a D chord barring at the fifth fret (**Example 20**) and at the seventh fret (**Example 22**) will give you G (IV) and A (V) chords, respectively—useful for slide. **Example 21** shows you some G-chord variations that utilize open strings, and **Example 23** does the same for the A chord.

Examples 24–26 will give you a little practice in playing an alternating bass utilizing the sixth and fourth strings. **Example 24** is the thumb-picked bass line that forms the backbone of the proceeding figures. **Example 25** adds notes on the top three strings, played in between the bass notes, and **Example 26** adds pinch on the first beat of the measure, as well as treble notes in between the bass notes.

Example 14

Example 15

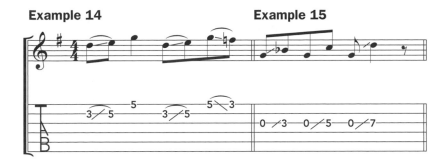

Tuning: D A D F♯ A D

Example 16

D minor pentatonic

Example 17

D major pentatonic

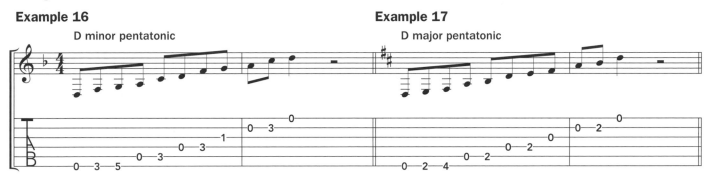

Examples 18–23

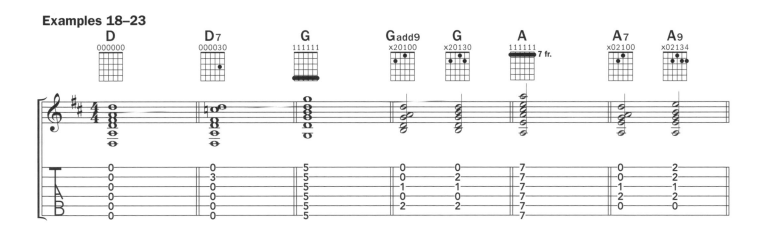

Example 24

D

Example 25

D

Example 26

D

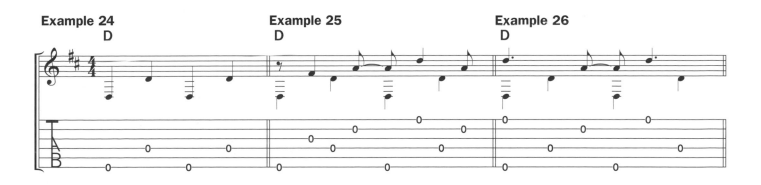

Charley Patton

Master the classic open-G bottleneck moves of the father of the Delta blues

Not enough can be said about the influence of Charley Patton, a musician who is widely considered the father of the Delta blues. He informally mentored none other than Robert Johnson, and Son House, Howlin' Wolf, Muddy Waters, Elmore James, and John Lee Hooker are just a few of the pioneering blues guitarists indebted to Patton.

Charley (sometimes spelled Charlie) Patton was born in 1891 near Bolton, in southern Mississippi. He was of a mixed racial background, a true American melting pot of African American, white, and possibly Native American blood. In 1897, his family moved to the Dockery Plantation, where he learned guitar from a fellow resident, Henry Sloan.

While living at the plantation, Patton met Henry C. Speir, a white music store owner who worked as a talent scout for several record companies and produced the important recordings of many Delta Blues artists. Beginning in 1929, Patton recorded several sides for Paramount records, including "Pony Blues," which became a hit and allowed him to establish a somewhat lucrative career.

Audiences all over the South soon packed in to witness Patton's flamboyant performances—he was known to play the guitar behind his back—matched with his loud, gravelly voice. He went on to record great tunes like "Banty Rooster Blues," "Green River Blues," "Shake It and Break It," "A Spoonful Blues," and many others before his untimely death in 1934 from a mitral valve disorder.

Patton's recordings can be a bit challenging because they suffer from the poor quality of the times. So I came to Patton's material not from the original sources but through modern players like Alvin Youngblood Hart, whose rendition of "Pony Blues" on his Big Mama's Door album captures the dynamics and rhythmic propulsion of the playing with much improved audio.

Patton played many styles, from deep blues to hillbilly songs to 19th-century ballads and other forms of country dance music. He achieved a bold sound by tuning his guitar up a step and a half, which gave his slide playing a bright and articulate panache. In this lesson, you'll look at how he played in open G, up a minor third (F B♭ F B♭ D F). You probably don't want to tune up so high, so play the examples in this lesson either with a capo at the third fret or simply in open G.

GETTING STARTED

Begin this lesson by tuning to open G. To get there from standard tuning, tune your sixth and fifth strings down a whole step, to D and G, respectively, and your first string down a whole step, to D.

In several songs Patton uses a similar strumming pattern that can be played in a couple of different ways. "Tom Rushen Blues," "High Sheriff Blues," and "Hammer Blues" share this same rhythm. In **Example 1a**, use a down/up/down/up/up/down pattern, playing the downward strums with your thumb and the upward ones with your index finger. **Example 1b** is another typical Patton pattern; play it using all downstrokes. These two patterns provide the rhythmic foundations for the examples that follow.

BOTTLENECK BLUES

Patton is believed to have played both lap-style slide (with a knife over the strings) and bottleneck. For this lesson, stick with bottleneck. It's not known which finger Patton placed the slide on, but I recommend using your fourth finger, allowing you to fret chords and play single-note phrases with your index, middle, and ring fingers.

If you're new to bottleneck playing, keep these pointers in mind: In general, heavier strings and slightly higher action work best with a slide. I prefer medium-gauge strings (.013–.056), but you can go thicker on the first and second strings. Some folks use a .015 or even .016 for string 1 and adjust accordingly for strings 2 and 3. Incidentally, it is thought that Patton used an unwound third string.

Try **Example 2**, a lick similar to those heard in "Tom Rushen Blues" and "High Sheriff Blues." The bass accompaniment is almost a monotonic pattern but with some gaps and other rhythmic flourishes. For instance, in the second measure the bass drops out and the slide takes over. These slide phrases should be played very quickly. To work up to this, practice sliding from the second to the fifth fret, as well as from the fifth to the seventh—and stopping on a dime.

Example 3 is similar to the main phrase in one of Patton's most famous songs, "Banty Rooster Blues." Again, most of the slide is played on the first string. Keep in mind that the slide notes trace the melody of the song and have a slightly clipped sound.

Tuning: D G D G B D

Example 1a
G

Example 1b
G

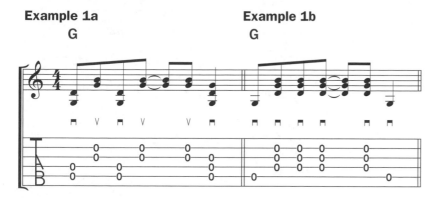

Example 2
G

with slide (all examples)

Example 3
G

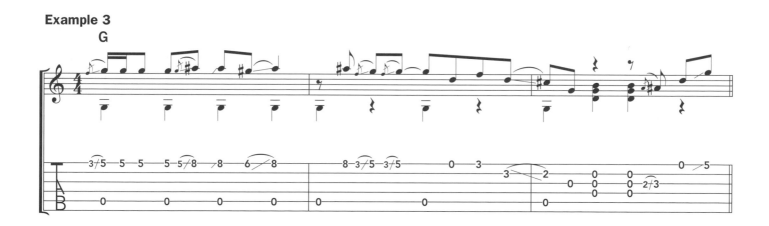

Another Patton classic, "Mississippi Bo Weavil Blues," serves as the inspiration for **Example 4**. This time the bass rhythm is centered on an alternating pattern that travels between the fifth and fourth strings, playing the chord's (I) tonic and (V) dominant. By now, you might have noticed that the G on string 1, fret 5 serves as an anchor for Patton's melodies.

In "Bo Weavil," Patton gives extra emphasis to the note by playing it an octave higher, at the 17th fret. This may have been one of the songs that he played lap-style with a knife blade. If you are having a tough time catching that 17th fret, reach up with your entire hand above the fretboard, so that you only need to glance the first string.

Example 5 shows how Patton often played the IV chord (C) in open G tuning. The bottleneck covers all of the strings and slides between frets 4 and 5. Make sure you keep even pressure along all the strings with your slide, otherwise you will get an audible—and unwanted—rattle.

In "Hammer Blues," approximated in **Example 6**, Patton takes another approach to the IV chord. He plays it using slides on strings 1 and 2 only. The succeeding single-string slide notes played on string 3, fret 7 imply a V chord (D). **Example 7** is similar to "Banty Rooster Blues." Here a single-string slide movement reflects a change from the V (D) to the IV (C) chords and then back to the I (G). Try directing your slide by tilting in to play strings 3 and 4, thus avoiding strings 1 and 2.

Example 4

Example 5

Example 6

Example 7

"LOW DOWN SHERIFF BLUES"

Example 8 is a tribute to Patton I call "Low Down Sheriff Blues." It starts off with the basic strumming groove from Ex. 1, then progresses through a series of slide runs, mostly on string 1. One of the keys to Patton's slide playing is to leave open spaces where the slide notes are not accompanied by the bass. For example, in bars 4, 8, and 11, the bass notes drop out. Also, most of the slide notes are played quickly, represented by grace notes (small ones).

Patton would sometimes make big leaps very quickly on the fretboard with the slide and stop suddenly—e.g., the slide from fret 2 to fret 8 on string 1 in bar 7. If these angular slides give you trouble, just isolate them and slow things down, gradually increasing the speed until you can play them fluidly—and with that certain panache.

Example 8
"Low Down Sheriff Blues"

G

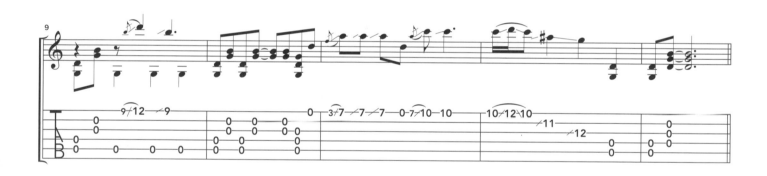

Elizabeth Cotten

Open tunings are key to sounding like the folk-blues fingerstyle legend

Few guitarists have had as much impact on fingerstyle folk and blues guitar as Elizabeth Cotten (1893–1987), the singer-songwriter whose songs have been covered by Bob Dylan, Joan Baez, David Bromberg, the Grateful Dead, and many others. Born in Chapel Hill, North Carolina, Cotten grew up in a musical family. She started off on her brother's banjo and then scraped up enough money to buy her first guitar, a $3.75 Sears & Roebuck model, which, being left-handed, she played upside down.

Cotten wrote her first songs, including "Freight Train," as a child, but gave up playing when she married and had children. She would have remained unknown if not for moving to Washington, D.C., where she found herself in the employ of the folk-singing Seeger family (Charles and Ruth Crawford Seeger), who encouraged her to reconnect with the guitar. Cotten was in her 60s when she began her recording and performing career.

The folk crowd drew inspiration from Cotten's songs in standard tuning, like "Freight Train" and "Mama, Your Papa Loves You," as well as her instrumentals in alternate tunings, like "Spanish Flang Dang" (in open G) and "Vastapol" (open D). Here's a look at some of the ideas and phrases that Libba, as she was nicknamed, would play in open G and D.

OPEN-G TUNING

To get into open G, also known as Spanish tuning, lower strings 1 and 6 down a step, to D, and string 5 down a step, to G. Cotten's "Spanish Flang Dang" serves as a good introduction to this tuning,

as the fretting-hand fingerings are straightforward, with only three chords (G, C and D7), all shown in **Example 1**.

Libba had an idiosyncratic picking hand, playing bass notes with her index finger and melody notes with her thumb (her alternating bass lines are known as Cotten Picking). Unless you're also playing upside down, you can use the more conventional picking pattern shown on the G chord in **Example 2** and on D7 in **Example 3**: Pick the bass notes with your thumb and the notes on strings 1, 2, and 3 with your ring (a), middle (m), and index (i) finger, respectively. But feel free to use any other fingerpicking pattern that works for you.

In "Spanish Flang Dang," most of the melodic movement occurs on the first string during the G-chord sequences. **Example 4** combines selected notes from the G-major scale (G A B C D E F♯) with the fingerpicking pattern from the previous examples. As for your fretting hand, play the fifth-fret G with your second finger, the seventh-fret A with your fourth finger, and the fourth-fret F♯ with your first finger.

Some of Cotten's more interesting touches came from her variations in picking and phrasing, like those seen in **Examples 5a–b**. Both figures start with a G chord that's rolled quickly, from lowest note to highest, with the thumb, index, middle, and ring fingers. But while Ex. 5a follows the roll with a slide, Ex. 5b uses a hammer-on.

Example 6 shows some transitions through the IV (C) and V (D) chords. Drag your thumb (p) through the eighth-note sequences and then return to a normal fingerpicking pattern for the quarter-note measures. In **Example 7**, apply a roll to the V chord, which transitions back to the I (G).

Tuning: D G D G B D

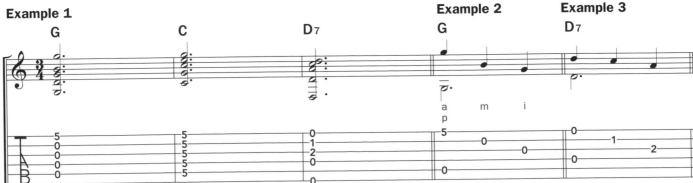

Example 4

Examples 5a–b

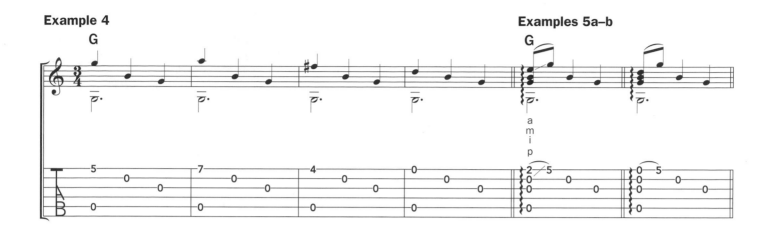

Example 6

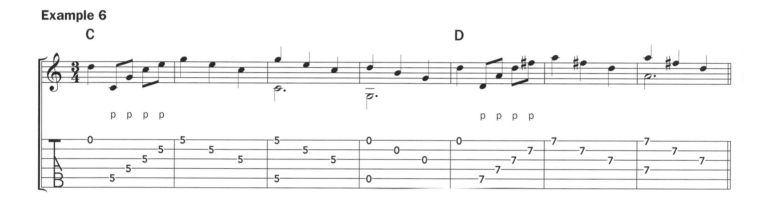

Example 7

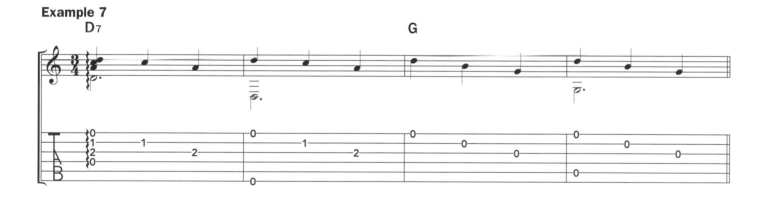

Tuning: D A D F♯ A D

Example 8

OPEN-D TUNING

Now try some ideas in open-D tuning (tuned low to high: D A D F#
A D) taken from her popular song "Vastapol." To get into open D
from open G, raise string 5 up a step, to A; lower string 3 a half
step, to F#; and lower string 2 a step, to B.

In performance, Cotten almost always varied her phrasing, yet
she followed the basic chord structure. In the key of D major, she
might have started out on the IV chord (C), like in **Example 8**.
Notice that the G chord has the third, B, in the bass, as this note
is easier to finger in open position than the root, which is on
string 6, fret 5.

Example 9 shows a variation that uses a slide from E to F#,
making for a quicker transition back to the D chord. Use your
second finger for fretting both the slide and the following

hammer-on. The hammer-on-and-slide motif is duplicated in
Example 10, this time going from the V chord (A7) to the I.

Cotten sometimes played "Vastapol" with a center section
similar to **Example 11**. The grace-note slides and hammer-ons
here create an infectious groove. Play the slides and hammer-
ons with your second finger. In a separate verse of "Vastapol,"
for the I chord, Cotten sometimes used a phrase like **Example
12**, featuring a common blues motif: a bend on string 2, paired
with a stationary note on string 1. Fret the bends with your
second finger, so that your other fingers are free to cover the
subsequent notes on string 1. Check your into-nation by playing
the ninth-fret F# on string 2 and listening carefully to the pitch.
Then bend the note at the eighth-fret F up a half step, making
sure to accurately hit the F#.

Example 9

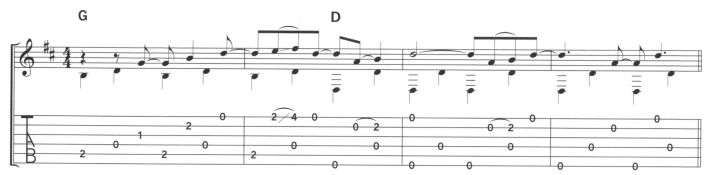

Example 10

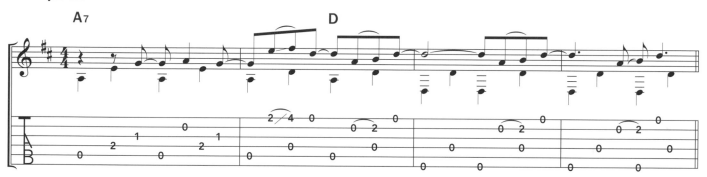

Example 11

Example 12

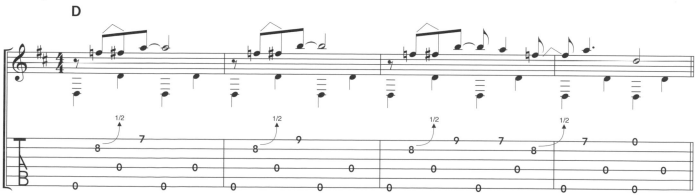

"LIBBA-RATION"

In **Example 13**, you'll find my tune "Libba-ration," inspired by "Vastapol." "Vastapol" is loosely built on 24-bar verses consisting of three eight-bar sections. Since Cotten's playing was somewhat improvisational and could change from performance to performance, I have taken some liberty with the structure. Instead of three eight-bar sections I've created one four-bar section and two-eight bar sections.

The first four bars are all built on the I chord. This section takes one of the motifs from "Vastapol" and expands on it with melody notes at frets 10 and 9 on the first string. The next eight-bar section travels back and forth between the IV (G) and I (D) chords. It has a call-and-response flavor with the same alternating bass for each chord.

The last eight-bar section echoes the previous eight bars but travels back and forth between the V (A7) and I (D) chords.

Slurs—bends, pull-offs, hammer-ons, and slides—are integral to the flavor of this piece.

You can pick any of the phrases from "Libba-ration" and use them as exercises for perfecting your technique. Hammer-ons that land on the beat with a bass note being played at the same time can be tricky because the heavier-sounding bass notes can swallow up the hammered-on notes. Resist the urge to separate the hammer-on from the bass. In measure 5 of "Libba-ration," for example, isolate the first two beats and practice them until you've got the timing correct.

Being a self-taught guitarist who played the guitar upside down certainly must have been a challenge for Elizabeth Cotten. You can take inspiration from her sheer will to learn the instrument. And—even without reversing the order of your stings—you can learn a lot by trying to capture Cotten's sound, phrasing, and dynamic approach to the guitar.

Example 13
"Libba-ration"

Memphis Minnie

The open-G stylings of an undersung fingerstyle blues artist

Lizzie Douglas, a.k.a. Memphis Minnie, was born in 1897 in Algiers, Louisiana. The eldest of 13 children, she learned to play the guitar at the age of 11 and was performing on the streets of Memphis, Tennessee, by the time she was 13. From 1916 to 1920, she toured with the Ringling Brothers Circus, and then wound up back on Beale Street in Memphis.

Memphis Minnie had a breakthrough in 1929 while performing with her then-husband, Joe McCoy, at a Memphis barber shop. A Columbia records talent scout heard the duo and invited them to New York to record. The pair, billed as Kansas Joe and Memphis Minnie, recorded and performed together from 1930 until 1935.

After divorcing McCoy in 1935, Memphis Minnie struck out on her own. Based in Chicago, she recorded and toured, mainly in the South. And she continued to play, and even recorded electric guitar on several tracks in the 1940s. All told, she recorded over 200 sides, including "When the Levee Breaks," "Black Rat Swing," and her biggest hit, "Me and My Chauffeur Blues."

By 1957, interest in her music had begun to wane, and Memphis Minnie, at age 60, retired from music. Three years later she suffered a stroke, which confined her to a wheelchair; her health continued to decline, and she passed away in 1973 at the Jell Nursing home in Memphis.

Memphis Minnie was a masterful guitarist who played intricate fingerstyle arrangements that accompanied her strong voice. Her early recordings, released in the 1930s, represent her finest playing. In this lesson you'll look at her playing in open-G tuning (low to high: D G D G B D), with examples based on the songs "Crazy Cryin' Blues," "Don't Want No Woman," and "Wild About My Stuff."

"CRAZY CRYIN' BLUES"

Examples 1–4 are inspired by "Crazy Cryin' Blues." The guitar parts here reflect the anguish and urgency of the vocals. If you play along with the original recordings, use a capo at the sixth fret.

In **Example 1**, over the I chord (G7) intro, Memphis Minnie plays a stock open-G line, but in the second bar she turns the triplet line into 16th notes, which increases the urgency. Note that on the recording there is a second guitar (played by Joe McCoy) in the mix, so it can be a little hard to distinguish the bass pattern, but an alternating bass line on strings 5 and 4 sounds appropriate enough.

In later verses of "Crazy," Memphis Minnie throws in some nice finger rolls similar to those shown in **Example 2**. The typical blues guitarist picks with the thumb and one or two fingers, but to execute the roll it's best to use your thumb (p), index (i), middle (m), and ring (a) fingers as shown in the notation. When playing this kind of roll, your picking hand should move as if you're turning a doorknob.

Example 3 demonstrates a typical move to the IV chord, with strings 1–5 barred at fret 5, and a descending line on string 1. Barre the fifth fret with your first finger and use your fourth and third fingers to stop the eighth- and seventh-fret notes, respectively.

Example 4 approximates the last three measures of "Crazy"'s 12-bar verse. Start out with a D7 chord, fingered the same way as in standard tuning, but with a slight change—the first string is open, rather than stopped at the second fret. Note how the notes on string 1 then ascend and descend through notes that include the ninth (E) and raised ninth (F/E#), adding a bit of sophistication to the proceedings.

After the D7 bar, you'll play a very cool G-chord run: Slide with your first finger, barring the top two strings, to imply a G7 chord that morphs its way into a G triad played on strings 2 and 3, fretted with the first and second fingers, respectively. Maintain that shape as you descend chromatically down to another G played on the open G and B strings.

"DON'T WANT NO WOMAN"

Examples 5–8 are based on "Don't Want No Woman," a duet with Kansas Joe. To match the pitch of the original recording, use a capo at the second fret. The opening line of the intro is shown in **Example 5**, which throws out a barrage of attention-grabbing double-stop triplets before settling into a more languid pattern in bar 2. This sets up the background for the first two bars of the verses, depicted in **Example 6**.

Tuning: D G D G B D

Example 1

Example 2

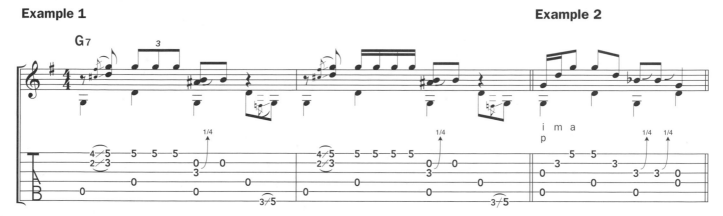

Example 3

Example 4

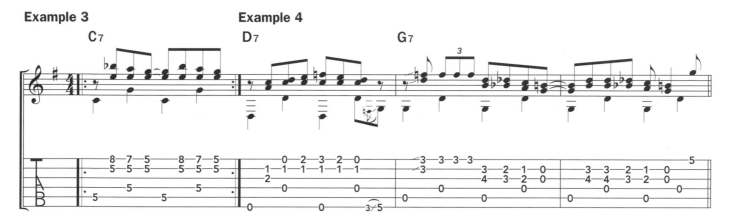

Example 5

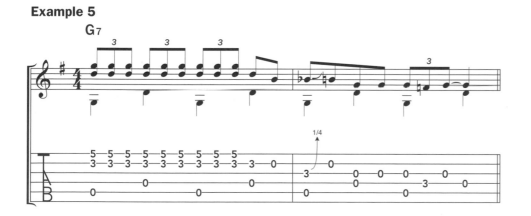

Example 6

OLIVIA WISE

The second two bars of Ex. 6 open up the guitar part as a response to the first two-bar vocal line. You might notice some similarity between these two bars and the G phrase in Ex. 4. When you study a player's style you will come to see these patterns and understand how his or her fingers travel the fretboard. Make note of these sections and you will gain valuable insights.

Example 7 shows how Memphis Minnie would play the IV chord in "Don't Want No Woman." In this voicing, she leaves the fifth string open, playing a G in the bass. She will use a similar approach for "Wild About My Stuff," which you'll look at in a moment.

The last four bars of a "Don't Want" verse are depicted in **Example 8**. Start with the same D7 chord you used in Ex. 4 and play another quick roll on beat 3 using p-i-m-a picking technique; grab the third-fret F on string 1 with your fourth finger. Play the same C7 chord with G in the bass from the previous example and finish off with a two-measure phrase on G.

Examples 9–10 are based on the hokum-style ditty "Wild About My Stuff." This playful song, with its double-entendre lyrics, has a fun guitar accompaniment that should put a smile on your face. Capo at the first fret to match the original recording.

In **Example 9**, the first four bars of the verse house a melodic phrase played between frets 2 and 5. I suggest dedicating one finger to each fret—first finger on fret 2, second on fret 3, etc. This will help you navigate the phrase without too much difficulty.

Example 10 uses your old friend the C7/G chord. Start this section off with only your first and second fingers fretting strings 2 and 4, respectively. Then, place your third finger down for the chord on beat 2—which happens to look like an A minor chord in standard tuning—and then, finally, the fourth finger to play the third-fret Bb on string 3. (Alternatively, you can extend your third finger to grab that Bb.)

Example 7

Example 8

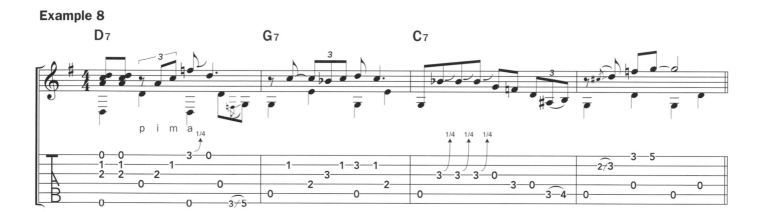

Example 9

Example 10

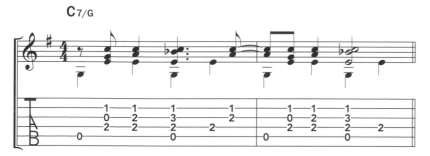

PUTTING IT ALL TOGETHER

Example 11 is a little piece I call "Minnie's G Blues." In the first bar I borrow a phrase from "Crazy Cryin' Blues," and create a response in the second bar borrowed from Robert Johnson's "Terraplane Blues." In the third measure I take the roll from "Crazy" and answer it with a simple descending run down the first string.

For the IV chord in measure 5, play the barre chord from Ex. 3 and then switch to the C7/G chord from Ex. 7, adding a third-fret D with your fourth finger on beat 2. Measures 7–9 are taken directly from "Don't Want No Woman," but in measure 10, to approach the IV chord from the V, I keep the F note as an echo of the previous chord. In the final two measures, return to G with a triplet-based double-stop and a single-string run that ascends from string 6 and culminates in a slide from G to the flatted seventh, F.

Memphis Minnie's guitar playing has gone mostly underappreciated through the decades, but for many blues-inspired fingerpickers she is a crucial link in the chain of Delta blues through to Chicago blues. Now that you have some of her ideas under your fingers, go out there and show some of your stuff.

Example 11
"Minnie's G Blues"

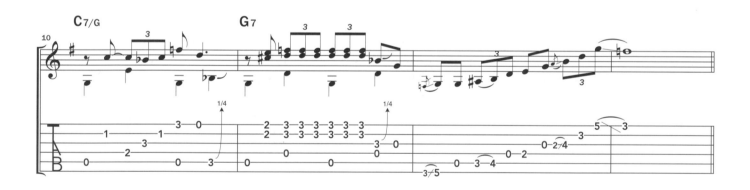

Son House

A guide to the intense stylings of the legendary Delta blues musician

Eddie James "Son" House (1902–1988) played and sang the blues as if he were possessed by demons. It might never be known whether this intensity was due to a conflict between his work as a bluesman and his role as a preacher or to some other phantom, but there is plenty of video footage from the 1960s to give you a taste of the power and intensity of his performances.

Son House was born near Clarksdale, Mississippi, and grew up with a musical father who played the tuba and drank heavily. Eventually, the senior House gave up the bottle and became a Baptist deacon. The younger House also took to religion and eschewed the blues until, at the age of 25, he heard a fellow musician playing bottleneck guitar and became obsessed. Not long after House began playing at juke joints and parties, a fight broke out at one of his performances, and he shot a man. He was sentenced to 15 years at the infamous Mississippi State Penitentiary at Parchman, but was released after just two years.

In late 1929, Son House crossed paths with bluesman Charley Patton, and the two performed and recorded together off and on until Patton's death in 1934. House eventually gave up music but was rediscovered by blues revivalists, who found him living in Rochester, New York, in 1964. He went on to perform with blues artists like John Hurt at venues such as the Newport Folk Festival.

From the 1960s on, House usually played a 1930s National Duolian. His style was a visceral mix of string popping, bottleneck slide, and dramatic physicality. Though he favored open tunings like G, D, and D minor, he sometimes used standard. In this lesson we'll focus on House's work in open G (low to high: D G D G B D). Remember, to get into this tuning, lower strings 1, 5, and 6 down a whole step from standard.

I, IV, AND V CHORD MOVES

House's best-known song, "Death Letter Blues," is the inspiration for **Example 1**—a passage anchored with a dead-thumb bass pattern and punctuated by single-string slide lines. Videos of House on YouTube reveal that the bluesman wore a bottleneck on his third finger and held the slide at a severe angle. Note that while this is fine for single-string lines, it's not ideal in terms of intonation for playing two or more strings at a time.

Example 2 reflects the I-chord (G7) phrases in the verses of "Death Letter Blues." Key to this figure is the repeatedly bent third-fret B♭. Nudge the string subtly, such that the pitch lands somewhere between the B♭ and B♮. This creates a nice tension between the major and minor third—a signature blues sonority.

In songs like "Death Letter Blues," "Jinx Blues," and "Low Down Dirty Dog Blues," House played IV-chord passages similar to the one demonstrated in **Example 3**. Here the chord's root, C, is played on string 5, fret 5. Note that House sometimes played the fifth (G) instead as the lowest note, on the open fifth string. To play Ex. 3, bar strings 1–5 at the fifth fret and use your third finger to grab the eighth-fret B♭. If this is too much of a stretch, wear your slide on your third finger and grab the B♭ with your fourth finger.

Example 4 depicts a move from the V chord (D7) to the IV and uses the same techniques as the previous figure. In **Example 5**, you'll see the I-chord phrases similar to what House played on "Jinx Blues." The bluesman was known for his prodigious snapping moves on the bass strings. To cop this approach, place your picking hand's thumb under the sixth string and snap or pop the strings—in this instance, as you play a smoothly descending bass line. I use the blade edge of a thumbpick to get underneath the string before picking. This makes for a dramatic rhythmic effect.

Two phrases inspired by House's intro to "Special Rider Blues" are shown in **Examples 6** and **7**. To play Ex. 6, ditch the bottleneck, maintain a steady bass pattern, and embellish the melodic phrases with finger slides and hammer-ons. Ex. 7 brings your bottleneck back into the fray. Notice the welcome change in texture that occurs after the first beat, when the bass drops out. A phrase on the upper strings takes over until the third measure, at which point it yields to a melodic idea on the lower strings.

Tuning: D G D G B D

Example 1

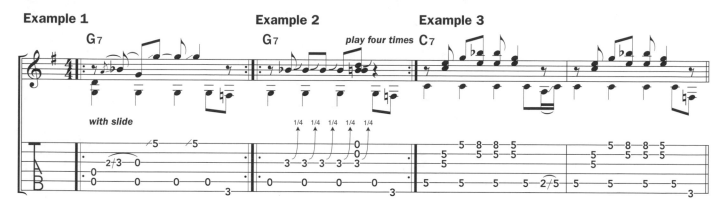

Example 2

Example 3

Example 4

Example 5

Example 6

Example 7

OLIVIA WISE

Example 8 is similar to the I-chord phrases in "Low Down Dirty Dog Blues." The slide lines are focused at the 12th fret and employ two and three strings. I would recommend forgoing technical authenticity in favor of intonational accuracy for this phrase. Remember, House's slanted slide sometimes gave him a slightly out-of-tune sound—forgivable, as his performances were so intense. To achieve pitch accuracy when playing Ex. 8, line your slide up with the given fretwire.

In **Example 9**, you'll learn a IV–V move similar to one House played in "Low Down Dirty Dog Blues." There's a nice juxtaposition between the down-stemmed bass notes, which are played squarely on the beat, and the up-stemmed notes, which are more rhythmically active.

Example 10 is based on House's version of "Walking Blues." Focus on the bass line, which uses a syncopated phrase and hammer-ons. In the third bar, after the repeat, play a slide phrase similar to that in "Death Letter Blues," and then move up to the 12th fret with the slide.

Example 8

Example 9

Example 10

"WALKING AND TALKING BLUES"

I've put House's ideas together in a 12-bar piece I call "Walking and Talking Blues" (**Example 11**). The first four bars combine the "Death Letter Blues" opening with the descending octave bass run from "Jinx Blues." Then there's a move to the IV chord in the fifth bar, leaving the fifth string open. I added a backward roll on the second beat of bar 6; pick this flourish with your ring (a), middle (m), and index (i) fingers.

In measure 7, for the return to the I chord, I have taken the B♭ microtonal bend from Ex. 2 and pitted it against the open B string to create tension. The move to the V chord in measure 9 is exactly like Ex. 4. Here I'm borrowing the C7 chord move from "Low Down Dirty Dog Blues" (Ex. 9). I finish things off with one more descending octave run, culminating in a bass-focused slide lick.

To really capture the essence of Son House's guitar style, it's best to go beyond the page and watch some of his performances. I would never suggest sacrificing accuracy, but intensity and passion are perhaps the most prominent characteristics of House's playing. Find a median between technique and emotion and you will be heading in the right direction.

Example 11
   "Walking and Talking Blues"

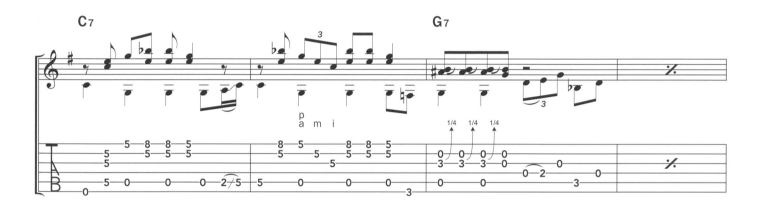

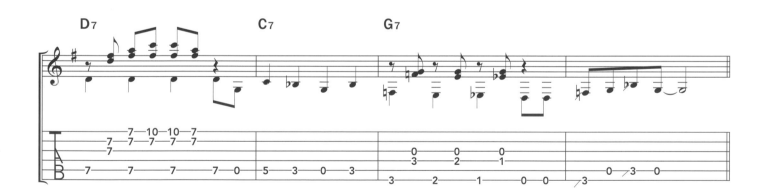

Skip James

An introduction to the Mississippi bluesman's haunting style

One of the most memorable scenes from the 2001 dark comedy *Ghost World* is one in which the protagonist, Enid, played by Thora Birch, listens to a vinyl recording of Skip James' "Devil Got My Woman." The alienation of the suburban teen is reflected in this haunting song.

Nehemiah "Skip" James (1902–1969) grew up on the Woodbine plantation near Bentonia, Mississippi. His early recordings, such as "Devil Got My Woman," "I'm So Glad," and "Hard Time Killing Floor Blues," all released in 1931, echoed the stark and harsh conditions of Depression-era life. The economic strife of the time led to poor record sales, and James was forced to relocate to Dallas, where he became a preacher.

In 1964 a group of blues revivalists, including the fingerstyle guitarist and composer John Fahey, traveled to Mississippi, where they found James lying sick in a hospital. With the help of Fahey and friends, James was able to perform and record until his death, in 1969. Thanks to notable performances at the 1964 Newport Folk Festival and the release of an album, *Greatest of the Delta Blues Singers*, James captured a new audience hungry to hear his evocative music. James' work is characterized by haunting themes, due in no small part to the use of open-D-minor tuning (low to high: D A D F A D). The guitarist picked up this tuning from a fellow Mississippi musician, Henry Stuckey, who had learned it from Caribbean soldiers while serving in France during World War I.

James used open D minor to create insistently repeating musical motifs, often based on just one or two chords, for hypnotic effect. I find his music challenging—not owing to any technical difficulties it presents, but because it's hard to capture the emotive quality of the milieu in which he worked. James' music always haunts me as I strive to articulate and understand it.

"DEVIL GOT MY WOMAN"

If you're familiar with open-D tuning (D A D F# A D), then it's very easy to get into D minor: simply lower string 3 down a half step, to F. In general, as you tackle these examples, it's best to dedicate your picking hand's thumb to the bottom three strings and your index and middle fingers to the higher strings.

Once you're in open D-minor, try **Example 1**, which is similar to the introduction to "Devil Got My Woman." James often used descending patterns like this, in which double stops are anchored by a steady bass pattern, to set up his verses. Your best bet is to play this example with your first and second fingers on strings 2 and 3, respectively.

Example 2 is patterned after a move further along in the intro to "Devil Got My Woman," where James skips strings and dispenses with the bass notes to give the triplet-based line a little more urgency. You can barre this figure with your first finger and use your third finger to grab that ninth-fret B.

For the verse of the same song, James shifts to an A minor chord, similar to the first two bars of **Example 3**, before moving back to D minor. Note that the second two bars provide an instrumental response to the vocal's call.

Example 4 is similar to the ending of "Devil Got My Woman" and is a relatively cheery departure from the rest of the song. Play this by barring the first three strings with your first finger. Pay attention to the triplet feel and syncopation.

Tuning: D A D F A D

Example 1

Example 2

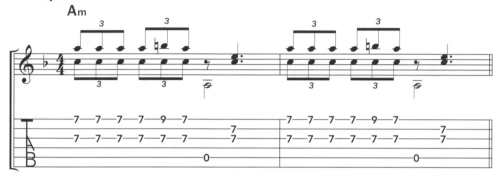

Example 3

Example 4

OLIVIA WISE

"HARD TIME KILLING FLOOR BLUES"

Example 5 is inspired by the introduction to "Hard Time Killing Floor Blues." Notice how the time signature—12/8, or 12 eighth notes to the bar—emphasizes the triplet feel and slow tempo of the song. If you have trouble understanding this meter, think of the first measure of the example as a shuffle, where the quarter note followed by the eighth note is one beat. The count is "One and, two and, three and, four," or long-short-long-short-long, etc. The dotted-quarter bass note in the second measure represents a full beat. The final three notes in measure 2 flow into the song's verse.

Underneath the main vocal line, James plays a pattern similar to **Example 6**. Again, getting the rhythm and feel for this passage is the most important thing. Look at each measure as combinations of triplets and shuffle, and you'll be on the right track. For instance, in the first measure, each group of three notes represents one beat.

Example 7 is a repeating phrase, similar to one under which James hums and moans in "Hard Time Killing Floor." The hypnotic effect on the original recording is practically unmatched on any other blues track of the era. To play the phrase, I recommend using your first finger on all of the third-string notes.

Example 5

Example 6

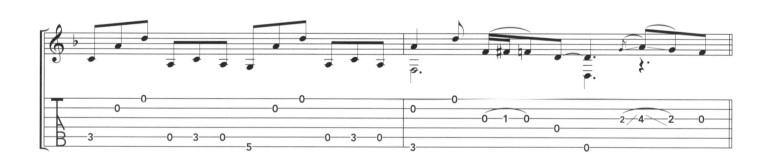

Example 7

"BAD TIMES COMING"

I've compiled this lesson's examples in an original piece I call "Bad Times Coming" (**Example 8**), which starts off with the "Devil Got My Woman" lick from Ex. 1. The fourth measure's phrase is similar to Ex. 2, but with a little more melodic movement on the second string. Use your first finger to barre the top three strings and a combination of your second, third, and fourth fingers to play the notes on string 2.

The phrase in measures 7–9 is all about the descending figure played on the second string with the open sixth and first strings surrounding it. Make sure to let the open strings ring to get an appropriately spooky sound. The last four bars of "Bad Times Coming" return to this phrase, but fleshed out with octaves between strings 2 and 5. Play the six-note chord on the first beat of each measure with a downward brush of your thumb.

As always, I recommend supplementing this lesson with a heavy dose of listening to the original recordings and internalizing the sounds and rhythms before sitting down to play. It's not necessarily a happy road, but it's a rewarding one.

Example 8
"Bad Times Coming"

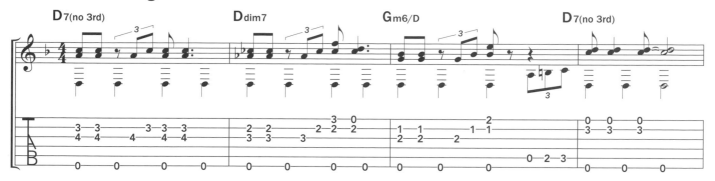

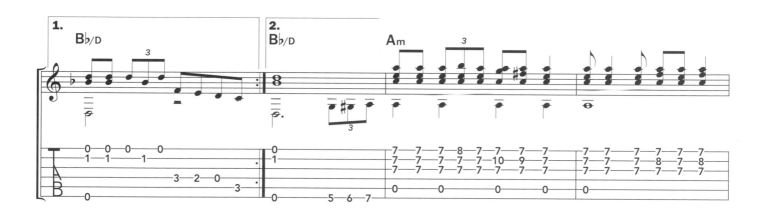

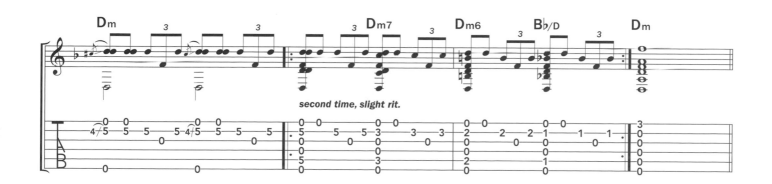

second time, slight rit.

Tampa Red

Learn how to play like "The Man with the Gold Guitar"

Tampa Red (1904–1981), born Hudson Woodbridge, in Smithville, Georgia, and raised as Hudson Whittaker by his grandmother, was one of the most popular bluesmen of the late 1920s and '30s. Sometimes billed as the "Guitar Wizard," he recorded over 250 songs between 1928 and 1942 and is known for his single-note bottleneck slide lines played on a National tricone resonator guitar.

After developing his guitar technique, Tampa Red moved to Chicago, where he got his big break by teaming up with singer Ma Rainey on several sessions. These dates led to a lasting musical partnership with Rainey's music director and pianist, Thomas Dorsey.

In 1928, Tampa Red and Dorsey recorded the hit song "It's Tight Like That," which helped launch the 1920s fad for hokum—a humorous style of blues filled with double entendres. The pair continued to work together until 1932, recording a total of 90 songs. After that, Tampa's output slowed a bit, but he continued to play on sessions with Sonny Boy Williamson, Big Maceo, Memphis Minnie, and others.

Tampa Red was one of the first blues musicians to play a resonator guitar. He was sometimes billed as "The Man with the Gold Guitar," based on his chosen instrument, a National Style 4 with gold plating. His fingerpicked style was clean and precise. Even on recordings from the 1920s, which can have notoriously bad audio fidelity, you can hear his phrasing very well.

If you're playing slide on a guitar with low action and/or light-gauge strings, you might have difficulty getting a satisfying tone when working through this lesson. Try some heavier strings—ideally, on a resonator—and you will get the best feel for Tampa Red's refined sound.

OPEN TUNINGS

Tampa Red played mostly in open-D (low to high: D A D F♯ A D) and open-E (E B E G♯ B E) tunings, using a capo to change keys. In this lesson, we'll focus mostly on moves inspired by two of his instrumentals in open D, "Denver Blues" and "Boogie Woogie Dance." These little masterpieces provide a good representation of Tampa's bottleneck slide style.

Examples 1–3 represent the first four measures of three different verses from "Denver Blues," which was originally recorded in open-E. To simplify things, I have written this lesson entirely in

open D. Everything is, of course, playable in either tuning, as the strings share the same intervallic relationship.

Rather than grounding his fingerstyle playing in a repetitive alternating bass pattern like Big Bill Broonzy or Mississippi John Hurt, Tampa intertwined the bass and treble voices more like Blind Blake or Reverend Gary Davis, employing a dance-like approach where the two voices would step back and forth with rhythmic emphasis.

The single-note slide phrases in these examples are mostly played on the first string. Make sure to keep your slide held low, so that it doesn't interfere with the open-string bass notes. By the way, Tampa Red wore his slide on his fourth finger. He also used a short slide, rather than one long enough to cover all the strings.

Example 1 introduces slide phrases that mostly follow the D major pentatonic scale (D E F♯ A B). Notice in measure 3 the triplet-based phrase that descends the string. Pick this run with your thumb and index fingers.

Taking its cue from the second verse of "Denver Blues," Example 2 reorders the phrase a bit, laying out another triplet-based run that hammers down on the fourth-fret F♯ then jumps up to the 12th fret. Practice this move slowly, until you can play it with precision, gradually edging up the tempo.

Example 3 ups the slide quotient while laying down a steadier bass pattern, played on the downbeat of the first three measures, to help ground you. Looking at notation while playing slide can be very challenging. For proper intonation, focus more on watching where your slide lands than the notes on the paper. Listen to these phrases closely and try to sing them before attempting to play them.

Tampa Red's shift to the IV chord was sometimes well-disguised—see Example 4, also inspired by "Denver Blues." In this two-bar section, there's not much harmonic information to indicate a shift to the G chord, save for the double-stop on beat 3 of bar 1. Of course, you don't necessarily need to hear the chord when auditory expectation has already mentally shifted your attention to it.

Example 5 is a turnaround similar to what Blind Blake would play in a tune like "Police Dog Blues." The phrase starts off on the D chord, then moves through G with a nifty triplet run in the bass. Then, there's a brief reset of the fretting fingers as you "stumble" through an A7 chord. I particularly like this broken-chord sound because the harmonic development is stretched out over an entire measure.

Tuning: D A D F♯ A D

Example 1

Example 2

Example 3

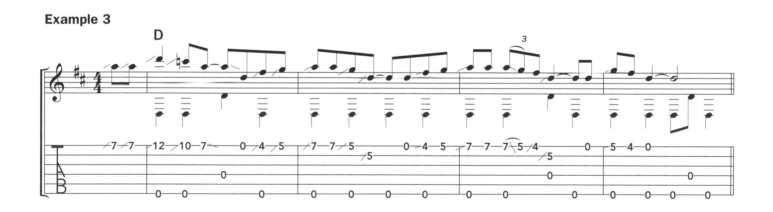

Example 4   **Example 5**

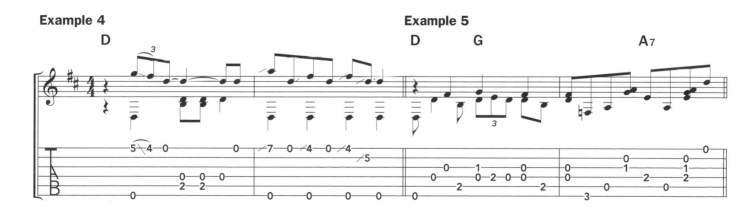

OLIVIA WISE

Taken at a faster tempo, **Examples 6–8** are similar to Tampa's "Boogie Woogie Dance." **Example 6** imitates the central groove of the song, a bit of a choppy sound with the interplay between bass and treble forming the dance on the I chord (D). The IV chord (G) comes into play in **Example 7**, similar to phrases Big Bill Broonzy played in songs like "Pig Meat Strut." The melody, which is played on beats 2 and 3 in the first measure, is pushed forward and played on beats 1 and 2 in the second measure. This creates an urgency that keeps things cruising along.

Based on the last four measures of a 12-bar blues, **Example 8** has a slick move starting on the V chord (A) and descending to the I (D). The chord grip in the first bar of this example is typical of an A chord voicing in D tuning—fingers 2, 1, and 3 on strings 4, 3, and 2, respectively. In the second measure, move this shape up two frets and place your third finger on string 1, then descend one fret. After that, play a series of descending octaves, culminating in a move back to D.

Example 9 is an imagined verse for "Boogie Woogie Dance." It blends single-string slide ideas over the I chord (similar to "Denver Blues") with chordal ideas for the IV and V chords. The song is anchored by a predominantly alternating bass line, with slide notes played on the first string. If you've mastered the slide phrases from the first three examples, you shouldn't have any problem with the first four bars of this example.

For the G chord in measure 5, use your third finger to play the descending melody on the first string. (Note: I have seen guitarist Toby Walker play this song with the slide on his third finger and use his fourth finger for melody.) In the descent from the A chord, I have given some picking-hand directions for a roll—remember: p = thumb, m = middle finger, and i = index. Strive to play these flourishes cleanly and with precision—again, hallmarks of Tampa Red's seminal style.

Example 6

Example 7

Example 8

Example 9

Booker White

Make your guitar sound like a locomotive in the style of this blues giant

K nown professionally as "Bukka" White, Booker T. Washington White played guitar like he was driving a train: his powerful alternating-bass grooves emulated the chug-chug of a puffing steam engine while his mournful slide produced the whines and whistles associated with the fading sound of a vanishing locomotive.

Born in Houston, Mississippi, White got his first guitar at age nine, a present from his railroad-working father. His first recordings appeared in 1930, under the name "Bukka" (though White preferred his given name); they combined country blues with gospel songs done in the style of Texas bluesman Blind Willie Johnson. In the 1940s, while serving time for assault at the infamous Parchman Farm Penitentiary, White was recorded by the folklorist John Lomax. Some of these recordings, including "Parchman Farm Blues," appeared on Harry Smith's influential folk-and-blues compilation *Anthology of American Folk Music, Vol. 4.*

In the 1960s, guitarist John Fahey wanted to track down White and sent a letter addressed to "Bukka White (Old Blues Singer), Aberdeen, Mississippi c/o General Delivery," hoping that the blues guitarist still lived in the town he had mentioned in "Aberdeen Mississippi Blues." The letter was forwarded to Memphis, Tennessee, where White was working in a tank factory. Fahey and White became friends. In 1964, White recorded the album *Mississippi Blues* for Fahey's Takoma label. The album introduced White to the folk-revival that was sweeping American college campuses.

White often played in nonstandard tunings like open G (low to high: D G D G B D), open D (D A D F♯ A D), and open D minor (D A D F A D), with copious slide accompaniment. His best-known songs include "Po' Boy," "Aberdeen Mississippi Blues," "Jitterbug Swing," and "Fixin' to Die Blues." White favored National single-cone resonator guitars, in particular the 1933 Duolian he called "Hard Rock," which added to the aggressive and percussive sounds he got in these open tunings.

In this lesson, you'll explore White's playing in open-G and open-D minor (sometimes referred to as "cross note" tuning). Keep in mind that White used a thumbpick and fingerpick on his index finger, his tempos were fairly quick (160–190 bpm), and that he was often brushing two or more strings with his thumb, producing a driving rhythm. Throughout the lesson, take it slow at first and work up the tempos as you feel more confident.

OPEN-G TUNING

Start in open G with a trio of examples from "Fixin' to Die." To get to open G (D G D G B D) from standard tuning, drop strings 1 and 6 a whole step, from E to D, and string 5 from A to G.

There are many versions of "Fixin'." **Example 1** is from a 1963 recording on which the tuning is dropped down a step-and-a-half to E and the tempo hovers around 190 bpm You'll notice that White could combine alternating bass and monotonic-bass in the same performance. Ex. 1 alternates the bass, travels back and forth between E and G in the treble and is a repeating pattern that sets up the groove. Play the figure with an open sound, strumming the strings with your thumb and index finger.

Example 2 uses a monotonic bass and is more subdued with the palm muting the strings. Allow the fleshy part of your picking-hand palm, closest to your pinky, to rest lightly on the bass strings. The 1963 version of "Fixin'" moves back and forth between these two grooves—these examples are a great place to start because they aren't too hard to play and you should be able to get the tempos up pretty fast.

In an earlier version of "Fixin'" White would play a short descending run punctuated by a slide note, like in **Example 3**. White used a metal slide on his pinky. His slide notes often occurred in flourishes—I believe the use of a thinner metal slide was important to his sound since it was easier to maneuver quickly and was less bulky than a thick glass slide. Make sure to slide right up to the fretwire at the fifth fret to get the proper intonation.

In **Example 4**, play full chords by placing the slide across five of the six strings. Many of White's songs were single-chord grooves, but "Po Boy" uses the slide at the fifth and seventh frets to play the IV (C) and V (D) chords, respectively. (Videos show that White performed this piece lap-style, using a nail for a slide, but you can play this example with the guitar in "Spanish" style.)

Start out with the G chord at the 12th fret and then play a cool lick that is useful whether you're playing solo or accompanying another player. The lick descends from the 15th to the 12th fret and then on to the tenth fret before moving to the C chord at the fifth fret. If you think of the 12th fret as home base for your G chord, you can move three frets up (to the 15th fret) or two frets down (to the tenth fret) for myriad licks that can be played on one or more strings. The same lick can be used to work your way down to the V chord (D) as shown.

Tuning: D G D G B D

Example 1

Example 2

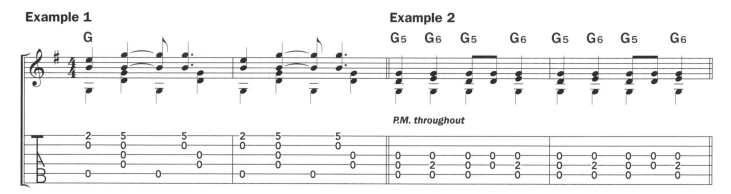

Example 3

Example 4

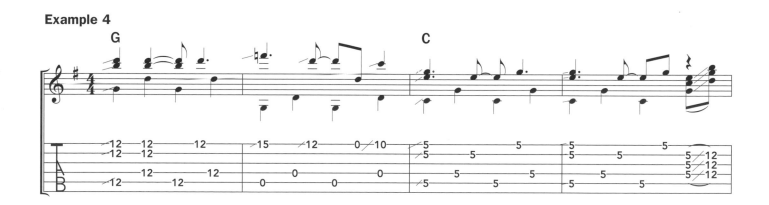

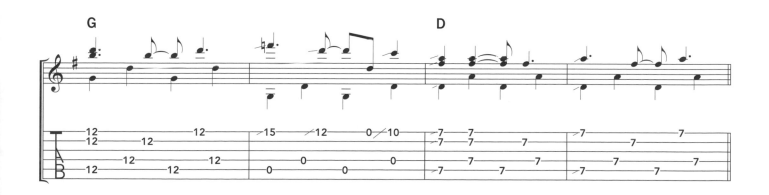

OLIVIA WISE

OPEN-D MINOR 'CROSS NOTE' TUNING

Unlike blues great Skip James, White didn't focus on the minor aspects of open-D minor tuning. Rather, he used the minor third, F, as a slur to hammer-on into the major third (F#), so that his playing in this tuning had more the flair of a major tuning.

To get to D minor tuning (D A D F A D) from open G, raise string 5 back to A; lower string 3 from G to F; and lower string 2 from B to A. **Examples 5** and **6**, inspired by "Jitterbug Swing" and "Aberdeen Mississippi Blues," show you how White rhythmically approached open-D minor. Both examples use an alternating-bass pattern. White often hammered from F to F#, with the latter note always landing on the downbeat, like in Ex. 5. This hammer-on,

from the minor third to the major third, creates a D major chord. As seen in Ex. 6, White sometimes started with the F# already fretted, but hammered on later, in the third bar of this figure.

Inspired by "Sic 'Em Dogs," first recorded as an inmate in the 1930s and his first known slide recording, **Example 7** has a slightly different bass pattern, which doesn't always alternate from string to string, but is hits steadily on the beat. **Example 8** highlights one of the flashier aspects of White's playing. He used this percussive expression on his recording of "Aberdeen Mississippi Blues" and it involves alternately tapping the guitar's neck and body while simultaneously hammering-on the fifth string at the second fret.

Tuning: D A D F A D

Example 5

Example 6

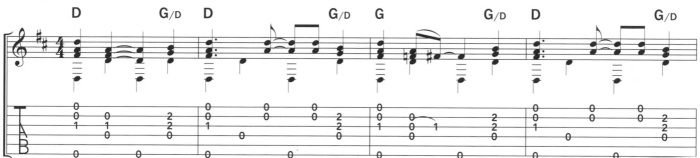

Example 7

Example 8

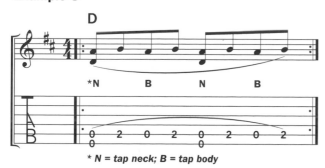

* N = tap neck; B = tap body

Example 9, which is patterned after "Jitterbug Swing," uses the bottleneck to create a call-and-response phrase over an alternating-bass pattern. Play this phrase with your slide held low, touching just the first string and slightly angled outward from the fretboard to avoid touching other strings.

It can be tricky to play slide in open-D minor, since you will want to avoid the third string. Use a finger—I prefer my first—to dampen the strings behind the slide. If you have good finger independence you can cover three strings or more with the dampening finger, while keeping contact with the slide on just the first string.

White would often make large leaps on the fretboard with the slide. **Example 10**, which takes its cue from "Aberdeen," starts out at the 12th fret, and then quickly moves to the fourth fret for a descending run. Play this slowly until you get the hang of this move, and try to avoid banging your slide into the fretboard, as I often did in trying to perfect it.

Example 11 is a short piece of mine called "June Bug Swing," which employs all the previously discussed examples and borrows several of White's open-D minor ideas. The opening four-bar sequence sets up the groove with an alternating-bass and hammer-on from the minor to the major third. That's followed by the tapping idea from "Aberdeen Mississippi Blues," but harmonized with the third string.

In bar 9, bring in the slide and play a phrase similar to "Jitterbug Swing," adding a major sixth to the tonality to fill in a portion of the D Mixolydian mode (D E F♯ G A B C). In bar 13, shoot up to the 12th fret with the slide to produce a quick double stop, adding some urgency to the sound. Finish things off with a return to the original groove. Once you get all the moves down, try playing this example at a brisk temp: 175 bpm or faster.

Working through Booker White's music is like a trip through groove land. It's especially gratifying if you lean towards fast, chugging tempos. If you're comfortable with playing an alternating bass in an open tuning, you can borrow many great ideas from this inspiring player. Try creating a groove or two from the above examples—you can embellish them with slide notes on other strings, or navigate to other parts of the neck. Let your blues muse free and get busy!

Example 9

Example 10

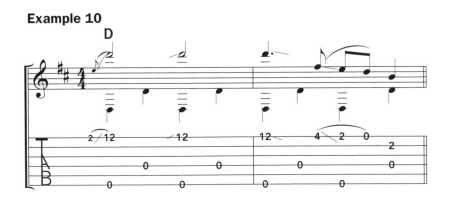

Example 11
"June Bug Swing"

Robert Johnson

Borrowing ideas from the great bluesman will enrich your musical vocabulary

Some think of Robert Johnson as the man at the crossroads with hell hounds on his trail, but many know him as the pre-war blues artist who had a profound impact on generations of musicians. His licks, phrasing, and general guitar panache have provided Eric Clapton, John Hammond, and many others the tools for creating inspired blues solos and rhythms. In this lesson, I'll take a look at some of the songs Johnson played in open tunings. The goal is not to play a particular song note-for-note, but to grab some of his melodic and rhythmic ideas and run with them in the context of a 12-bar blues.

GETTING STARTED

Johnson actually played closer in pitch to open-A tuning, but since that might add too much tension to your guitar neck, I'll go a whole step lower with open G (D G D G B D). **Example 1** demonstrates a common I–IV–V shuffle progression in the tuning. The standard treatment for the shuffle is to play two strings simultaneously, progressing from dyads containing the root and fifth (G and D) to the root and sixth (G and E) and root and seventh (G and F), with the consecutive eighth notes played not straight but long-short.

Johnson employed this style of bass-driven playing from time to time, but more often he would break up the sound. For instance, in **Example 2**, which is similar to a motif in his "Terraplane Blues," the I chord sounds quite different. It still starts out with the low-bass sound courtesy of the fifth and fourth strings, but then jumps to the higher strings, hitting G-type chords.

In **Example 3**, play the IV chord by barring strings 1–4 at the fifth fret and grabbing the eighth-fret B♭ with your fourth finger, or

if you're wearing a slide, your third finger. Then, perform a rhythmic flourish by bouncing on and off the first three strings at the fifth fret and landing back down on the original chord. To get a clean sound, pick the notes with your thumb and fingers, rather than strumming with a pick.

Example 4 is a cool riff, similar to "Terraplane." It's based on a compact G7 chord played on the top three strings. Beat 2 of this measure has more of a triplet feel. At the end of the bar, try a rake: drag your thumb or thumb pick down through the strings while palm-muting—keep your pick hand covering the strings near the bridge of the guitar to get a muffled sound—then pick string 2 with your index finger before bringing your thumb down heavily on the G-D dyad at beat 1 of the next measure.

SLIDE GUITAR TECHNIQUE

For the most part, Johnson used a slide sparsely, to punctuate phrases or reinforce vocal lines. A case in point is the pattern he played in "Walking Blues" (similar to Son House's "Death Letter Blues"), which informs **Example 5**. This riff is based on a monotonic bass pattern. The slide plays the in-between notes on the "ands" of 1 and 2.

Typically, in open G tuning, the IV chord would be played at the fifth fret, but Johnson sometimes used his slide to play it at the eighth fret, with just the fifth (G) and flatted seventh (B♭ creating a nice tension in the sound—see **Example 6**. And when playing the V chord, Johnson would often just play the root note with the slide like in **Example 7**, which is inspired by "Crossroads."

Tuning: D G D G B D

Example 1

Example 2   **Example 3**

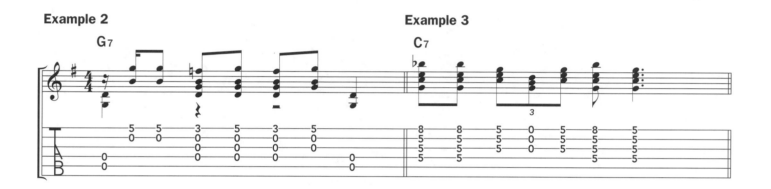

Example 4

Example 5   **Example 6**   **Example 7**

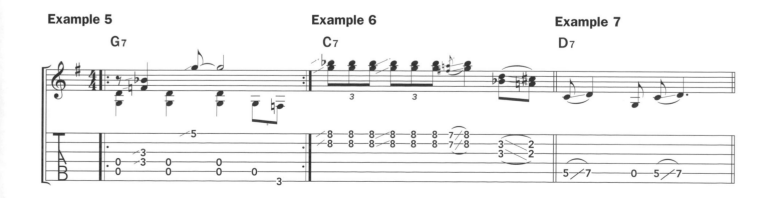

The 12th fret is prime real estate for some tasty slide work. Johnson used this position as home base for such melodic phrases, as in "Come on in My Kitchen," or a rhythmic statement similar to that shown in **Example 8**. He might play a triplet-based multi-string lick—think "Crossroads" or "Dust My Broom"—then stop dead in his tracks with a fretted (no slide) note like the low G in this example. This choppy style of playing helps accentuate the rhythm.

Example 9 ends a phrase typical of a song like "Come on in My Kitchen." This is a great lick that uses the fourth string to start off a bass-driven run culminating in the higher G note played at the fifth fret on the first string.

MASTER THE TURNAROUNDS

The turnaround is usually played in the last two measures of a 12-bar blues. Its purpose is to direct the music to return to the beginning of the progression, often via a phrase traveling from the I chord to the V chord. Johnson's turnarounds were often little works of art in themselves.

Example 10 is a simple descending turnaround that uses the open third string as an every-other-note drone, pitted against notes on the fourth string that descend from G to D. Incidentally, you can play this exact same turnaround in standard tuning if you are in the key of G. **Example 11** incorporates the sixth string to create a fuller sound. Use your bottleneck for the triple stop in the second measure.

Example 8

Example 9

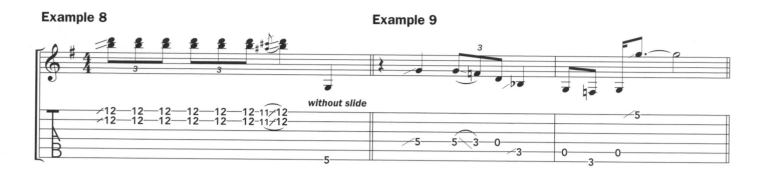

Example 10

Example 11

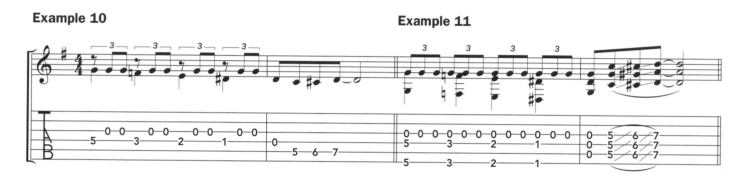

"THE R.J. WAY"

This piece (**Example 12**) uses Robert Johnson–inspired licks to create a solo comprised of two 12-bar choruses. The first four bars alternate between a standard two-string shuffle rhythm and two rhythmic variations. The first variation is taken from Ex. 2. The second is my own idea using the flatted seventh (F) played on the fourth string and descending to the fifth (D). The C chord in the bar 5 uses the same fingering as Ex. 3 and then bar 6 brings the slide into play.

The slide stays busy in measures 7–10, with licks at the 12th fret over the G chord, and then single-string slide lines for the V and IV chords before the appearance of the turnaround—a variation on Ex. 10, with three string rolls instead of an every-other-note drone.

The second 12-bar chorus starts in bar 13 with a nod to the "Terraplane Blues" lick from Ex. 4. I've played around with the phrasing by creating more of a shuffle eighth-note feel in the treble voicing of the second measure, and then a backwards triplet roll in the bar 15. In bar 16 the bass drops out, allowing the punctuating single note lick to stand on its own. Moving to the IV chord in bar 17, let the bottleneck slide from one fret below the chord and use percussive "chucks" to create a bit of separation.

Bar 19 returns to a single-note slide run at the 12th fret, using the 11th fret to create an evocative whine, like in "Come on in My Kitchen." Play another single-note slide phrase similar to the one in the previous 12 bars for the V chord and then a three-string C7 voicing that descends chromatically down to a C triad at the fifth fret. Finally, use the bass-driven turnaround lick from Ex. 11 and finish off with a slide lick that ends on the flatted seventh (F).

Try creating your own licks and variations from these examples. A teacher once told me that when you are improvising and stuck for an idea, think, "What would so-and-so do?" Fill in so-and-so with the great players like Johnson, as well as Skip James, Big Bill Broonzy, and Blind Blake, and you'll never be left wanting for ideas.

Example 12
"The R.J. Way"

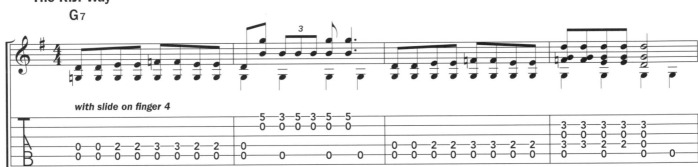

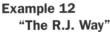

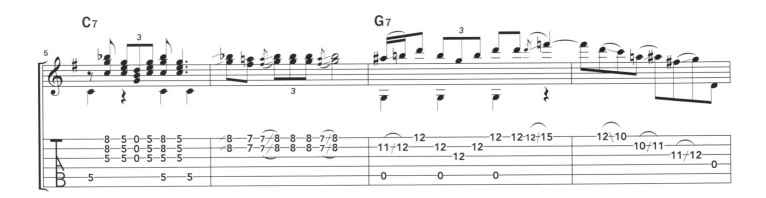

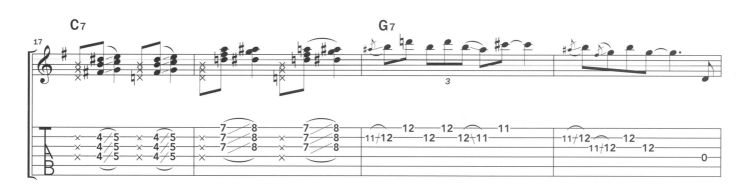

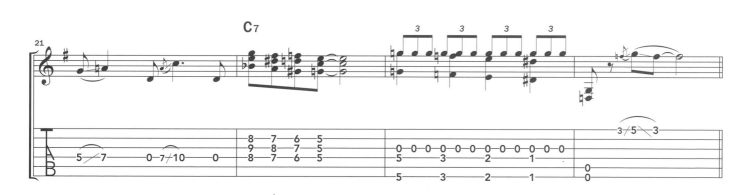

R. L. Burnside

Work out on single-chord grooves like the Mississippi hill-country blues master

The late Mississippi Hill Country blues artist R. L. Burnside was relatively unknown until the 1990s, when he signed with Fat Possum Records and began touring both nationwide and in Europe. His sound was heavily influenced by his neighbor, Mississippi Fred McDowell, as well as contemporary blues artists of the day, like Muddy Waters, John Lee Hooker, and Lightnin' Hopkins. Burnside's raw single-chord-driven and percussive sound was emblematic of the groove-driven Hill-Country players.

If you like your blues with funky drive (think Gary Clark Jr.), listening and learning Burnside's riffs and licks will get your mojo working. Make sure to check out Burnside's playing on YouTube, or on his many recordings, where you will find some great examples of how he approached the music.

OPEN-G GROOVES

Burnside played many of his tunes in open-G tuning (low to high: D G D G B D) with a funky vibe and percussive attack. Guitarists tend to gravitate toward his version of "Poor Black Mattie"—an infectious, single-chord groove that keeps the foot tapping.

Burnside relied heavily on single-chord grooves, and all of the examples in this lesson explore the possibilities of a single-chord groove in G. **Example 1** is inspired by the main groove from "Poor Black Mattie." The key to playing it is to nail the percussive "chucks"—like a rock drummer's snare hits—on the second and fourth beat of each measure. Burnside played fingerstyle, using mainly his thumb. To cop his sound in Ex. 1, use your thumb to brush the strings while simultaneously palm muting the bass strings—remember, allow your picking-hand palm to rest gently on the strings near the bridge. As for your fretting hand, play the notes on strings 1 and 2 with your first finger.

Example 2 is a slight variation on the "Poor Black Mattie" groove, which, after a slide up from the first to the third fret, has your third finger reaching for the fifth fret, G. Both Exs. 1 and 2 are faster grooves—around 160 bpm—and sound best played that way. It may take some time to nail these examples with the proper attack, but you should be able to get them grooving with a little practice.

In contrast, **Example 3**, similar to "Peach Tree Blues," is a much slower groove at around 100 bpm. This relaxed tempo is an invitation to play a couple more notes—and that's just what Burnside does. Slide on the second string with your third finger and play the fifth-fret notes with your first finger.

Example 4, inspired by "Skinny Woman," is also a slower groove that emphasizes the bass notes. Burnside, a master of transitions, would often morph a pattern like Ex. 4 into a riff like Ex. 3, before moving into a percussive palm-muted section like **Example 5**. On beats 1 through 3 of Ex. 5, use a down/down/up strumming pattern—your thumb on the downstrokes and your index finger on the upstrokes—while palm muting.

You can hear a John Lee Hooker influence in **Example 6**, which takes its cue from "Jumper on the Line." Burnside plays a boogie-style groove in his own percussive fashion. Check the notation for proper strum direction—again, use your thumb for the downward strums and your index finger for the upward strums.

Another great slow groove is "Rollin' and Tumblin'," which Burnside may have picked up from McDowell. For slide, Burnside placed the bottleneck on his ring finger. The syncopation of the slide phrases in **Example 7** is important. The first slide of the double stop on strings 3 and 4 is a little longer than the other slide notes. It gets a full eighth note, as opposed to a triplet eighth, so be sure to elongate the first slide double stop.

In **Example 8**, insert the opening phrase from "Rollin' and Tumblin'": a double-stop played on the first and second strings, which then transitions to the midrange groove from Ex. 7. Keep your slide low and evenly angled over both strings, as it's easy to misgauge your slide angle and not make good contact with the strings.

Tuning: D G D G B D

Example 1

Example 2

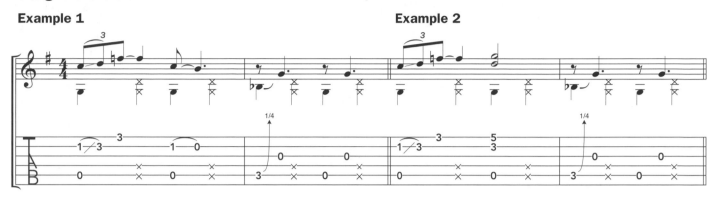

Example 3

Example 4

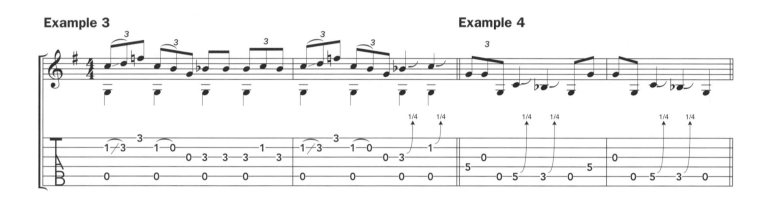

Example 5

Example 6

Example 7

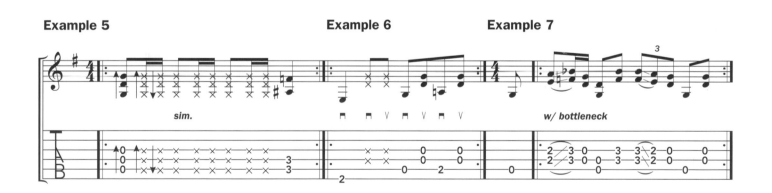

Example 8

OLIVIA WISE

NOW PUT IT ALL TOGETHER

In my original composition "Burnside's Brush" (**Example 9**), I borrow some of Burnside's licks and phrasing, while keeping the groove going strong. I wanted the transitions to sound natural, in keeping with Burnside's seamlessness.

Start off with the pattern from "Peach Tree Blues," keeping a slow and even pace. Play the slide notes with your third finger, not the bottleneck. In bar 4, bring in the bottle-neck to play a phrase similar to the bass-driven "Skinny Woman" lick, but with a triplet bass/treble/bass snap to punctuate the line. Use your thumb on the sixth string and grab the first and second strings with your middle and ring fingers, respectively.

After repeating the first six bars, climb up the neck a little to create a phrase that can either be interpreted as an extension

of the I chord (G) or as a move toward the IV chord (C). It might be a bit of a stretch, but use your third finger to reach up to the eighth fret.

In the next section, starting in bar 13, play a percussive/palm-muted triplet-based phrase that is punctuated by the same slide line from the second section. Then, perform a series of double-stops on the third and fourth strings that are similar to the groove from "Rollin' and Tumblin.'" Keep your slide tilted inward to get good contact with strings 3 and 4.

If you're a fan of R. L. Burnside, then you're already familiar with his strong rhythmic prowess. His picking-hand dynamics are equally important, and you can learn to copy them through careful listening. But most important, always remember to tap your foot and stay in the groove!

Example 9
"Burnside's Brush"

Jimmy Page

Learn to play open-G slide like the legendary Led Zeppelin guitarist

As Led Zeppelin's musical architect in the late 1960s and '70s, guitarist and songwriter Jimmy Page created sound tapestries that musicians continue to mine. Page has said that with the seminal British blues-rock band he was mixing the light with the dark, and many of Zeppelin's albums feature pounding rock with softer touches of acoustic folk, blues, and Middle Eastern influences.

He was born James Patrick Page on January 9, 1944, in Heston, Middlesex, England. Page picked up his first guitar when he was 12 years old and was mostly self-taught. His earliest musical inspirations were rockabilly guitarists Scotty Moore and James Burton, who played in Elvis Presley's band, as well as blues players like Elmore James, Freddie King, and Hubert Sumlin.

In the mid-1960s, Page became an in-demand session musician in London and eventually replaced ace guitarist Jeff Beck in the Yardbirds. When that band fell apart, Page and a fellow session player, bassist John Paul Jones, found two willing coconspirators in vocalist Robert Plant and drummer John Bonham. This quartet would become Led Zeppelin.

In Led Zeppelin, Page borrowed from the blues to create memorable songs like "When the Levee Breaks," "Since I've Been Loving You," and "In My Time of Dying." In addition to standard tuning, he used alternate tunings like open C, DADGAD, and open G. In this lesson, I'll focus on Page's blues-oriented work in open G. Though he recorded some of this work on electric guitar, all of the examples sound equally good on acoustic or resonator, and are best played with a flatpick.

THE NUTS AND BOLTS

The first four examples here are inspired by "When the Levee Breaks," from Led *Zeppelin IV* (1971). **Example 1** is similar to the song's droning groove. Double-stop pull-offs and open strings keep the droning quality fluid and steady.

The break between verses is approximated in **Example 2**. Pull out your bottleneck slide—Page uses his ring finger—to play this figure, with its E♭, C, and F chords leading into a syncopated line played with C, B♭, and G chords. **Examples 3 and 4** are similar to the second breaks in "Levee." On the original recording, Page plays these single-string phrases on the first two strings—overdubbed and positioned underneath full chords. Keep your slide directed low, so you are covering only the first two strings.

The intro to "Traveling Riverside Blues" is the prototype for **Example 5**. Page returns to a phrase like this throughout the song. Note that the example has a bit of an Elmore James/"Dust My Broom" kind of feel. After playing the multistring slide with the bottleneck at the 12th fret, jump to the third and fifth frets and open strings. Play the barred B♭ and C chords with the bottleneck, and then use your index or middle finger to play the descending turnaround phrase that suggests a chord progression of G7/F–Em–G/D–G/C–G.

Example 1

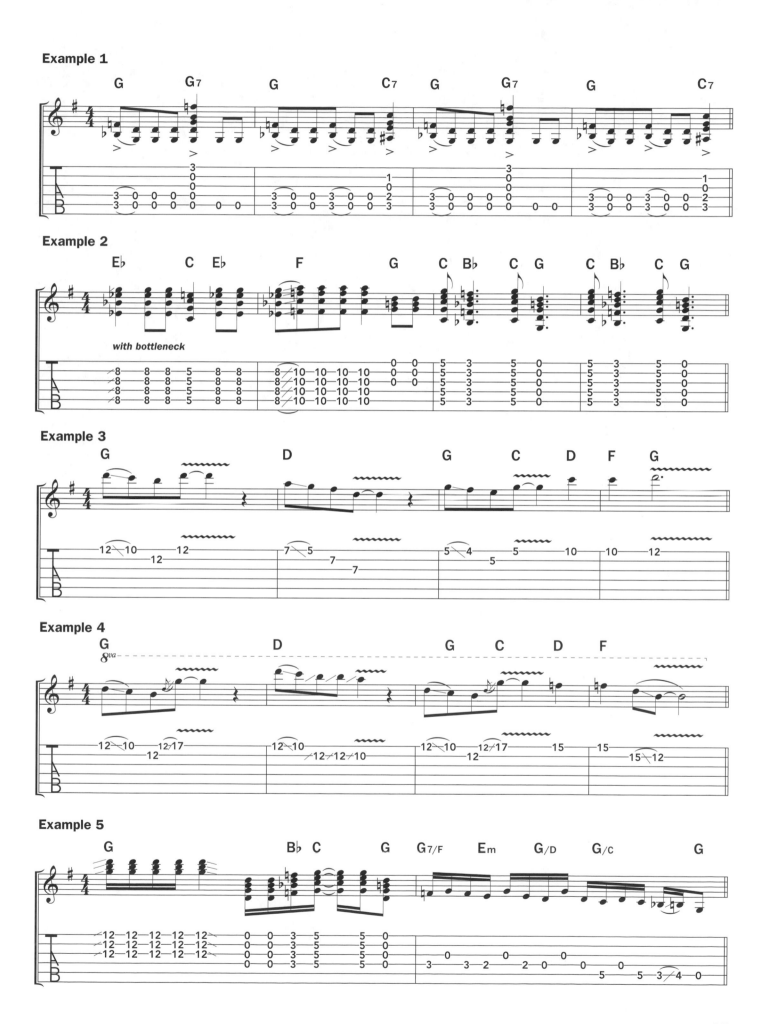

Example 2

Example 3

Example 4

Example 5

Example 6 is similar to what Page played for the I chord (G) in the verses of "Traveling Riverside Blues." It's a fairly common blues move of walking up the fourth string in open-G tuning to produce G, G6, and G7 chords, with an unexpected higher-register G7 punctuating the line.

Two approaches for negotiating the song's IV chord (C) are shown in **Examples 7 and 8**. Ex. 7 is similar to what you might hear Robert Johnson or Son House play, with a barred fifth fret and 6 and 7 chords played up the first string by adding the third and fourth fingers, respectively. But Ex. 8 is a little more like what Johnson would play for the I chord on a song like "Terraplane

Blues"—moving the figure up to the 11th and 10th frets on the second and first strings produces a C7 instead of a G7.

Examples 9–11 are patterned after parts of "In My Time of Dying," from the double album *Physical Graffiti* (1975). The languid approach to the bottleneck-produced dyads and triads in **Example 9** sets up the dire feel of this song. **Example 10** has a call-and-response flavor with the slide notes played on the third string answering the barred chords (played with slide) of the first measure. In **Example 11**, a repeating phrase is varied slightly each time—a prodigious use of navigating the third string with the slide.

Example 6

Example 7

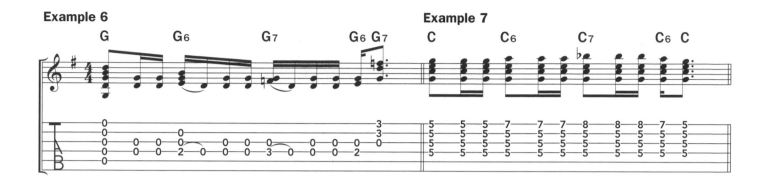

Example 8

Example 9

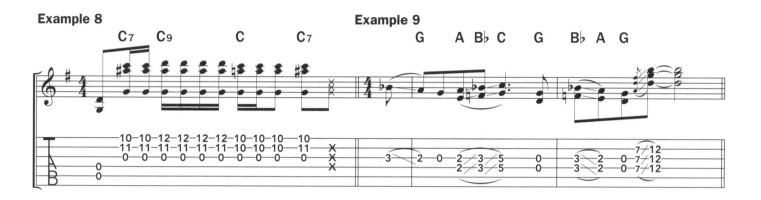

Example 10

Example 11

PUTTING IT ALL TOGETHER

I have put some of the licks from above to use in a 12-bar etude (**Example 12**). The opening phrase is a slight variation on the first lick from "When the Levee Breaks," using a quick slide on the sixth string to accent the droning quality. Play this slide with your finger rather than the bottleneck, which will keep the sound even and prevent the bottleneck from interfering with the notes played on the fifth and fourth strings. While you are directed to play this phrase three times, you can repeat it as desired for a trancelike effect.

In the next four measures is a variation on the phrase from Examples 3 and 4. In the third bar of this sequence, I have opted for a descending line that traverses the G minor pentatonic scale (G B♭ C D F) from a higher octave to a lower one and is then punctuated with a G7 chord like the one from Ex. 6. The following E♭–F–G chord sequence is taken directly from Ex. 2, and the last bit recreates the descending line from "Traveling Riverside Blues," but in eighth-note triplets, rather than 16th notes.

Jimmy Page is a master of taking old blues stylings and repackaging them to suit his artistic needs. In a nod to the tradition in blues of making it your own, Page stands out as a great example of being open to all possibilities. Get these riffs and musical ideas under your fingers and then take them somewhere new and exciting.

Example 12

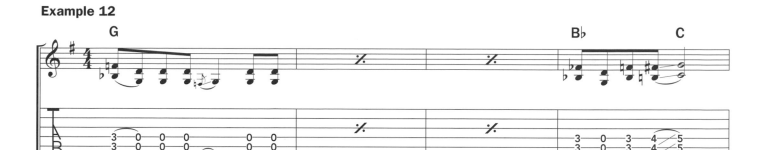

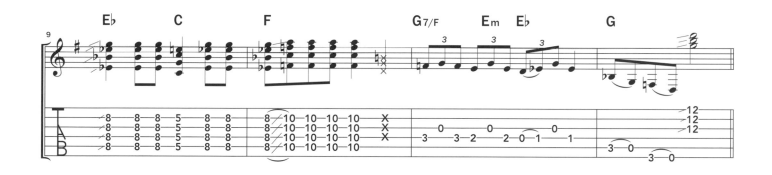

Kelly Joe Phelps

Exploring the modern blues master's slide work in open tunings

Kelly Joe Phelps is the total package. He's not just an excellent guitarist and singer, but a songwriter of depth and complexity. Prewar blues is just a stepping-off point for Phelps' intricate fingerpicking and soulful vocals; his guitar style is rooted in alternating-bass picking but extends far beyond, with a range of other syncopated approaches.

The depth of Phelps' musicianship perhaps owes to his unusual trajectory as a musician. Prior to becoming a blues-inspired fingerpicker, he was a bassist, heavily influenced by postbop and free jazz musicians like Ornette Coleman, Miles Davis, and John Coltrane.

Ever since his first recording, 1995's *Lead Me On*, Phelps has experimented with open tunings and slide techniques. He initially played lap style, in open D (low to high: D A D F♯ A D), but more recently has taken to playing bottleneck style (on a National Style O), in open G (D G D G B D).

In this lesson you'll adapt Phelps' open-D ideas to bottleneck style, with some examples inspired by "The House Carpenter" (from 1999's *Shine Eyed Mister Zen*). Then, you'll delve into his open-G work with some figures like those heard on 2012's *Brother Sinner & the Whale*.

Because Phelps' playing flows so hypnotically, you can be lulled into thinking it's easier to play than it really is. So take your time in learning his techniques—highly useful bottleneck moves, regardless of your style.

OPEN-D TUNING

"The House Carpenter" is built around a classic alternating-bass pattern on strings 6 and 4, taken at a brisk tempo of 225 bpm.

When you play the single-string slide notes in **Example 1**, hold the slide low, just covering the strings you are playing.

Example 2 is similar to a lick from one of the many guitar breaks in "The House Carpenter." It stretches up to the 15th fret, which might be a bit of a reach for a bottleneck player, especially if your neck joins the body at the 12th fret. But it's fine to use your entire hand above the neck to make the occasional long reach with your slide.

Examples 3a and 3b demonstrate two approaches to playing the same lick. Both examples use a double pull-off at the 15th fret, produced with the slide. In 3a, punctuate the lick with a double-stop at the 17th fret, but in Ex. 3b, play the same notes without the slide, on string 2/fret 14 and string 3/fret 13—a position that's easier to access for most bottleneck players.

OPEN-G TUNING

Now switch to open G to explore a few examples inspired by Brother Sinner & The Whale. Examples 4–8 are built from an alternating-bass backdrop on strings 5 and 4, and, occasionally, string 6. In **Example 4**, inspired by "Down to the Praying Ground," start out with your slide covering strings 1 and 2, landing on the flatted seventh (F♮) on the "and" of beat 1. Then move to the third string and perform a backward slide.

The last two bars of Ex. 4 are based on what are open-C-type shapes in standard tuning, but which take on more colorful sounds in open G—namely C7, with the fifth (G) and then the flatted seventh (B♭ in the bass, and Fmaj9, a sonority seldom heard in bottleneck blues. Start out bar 3 with your first and second fingers on strings 2 and 4, respectively, and keep these fingers held through the end of the next measure.

Tuning: D A D F♯ A D

Example 1

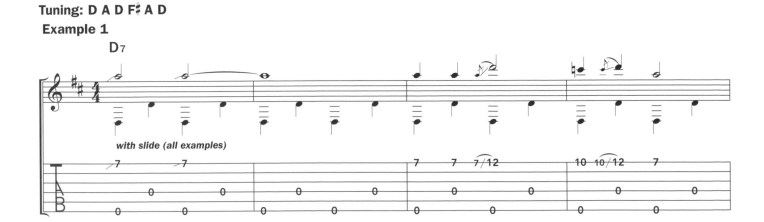

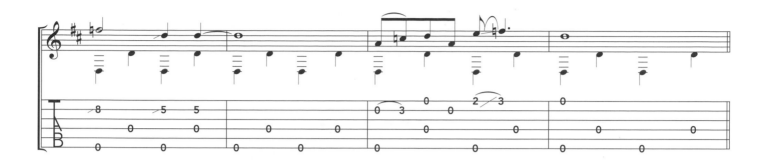

Example 2

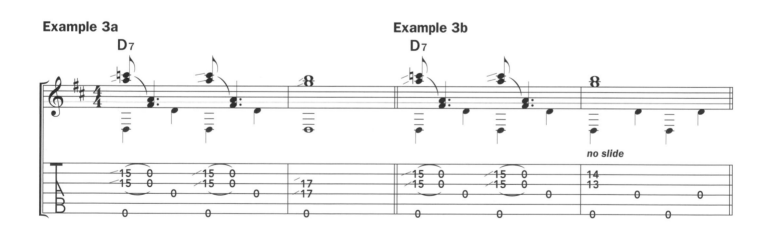

Example 3a

Example 3b

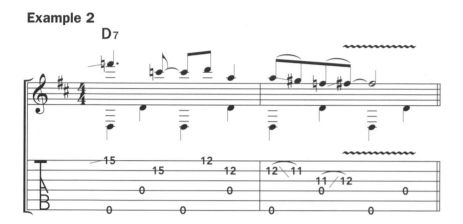

Tuning: D G D G B D

Example 4

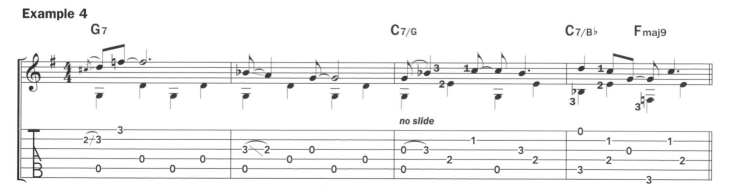

The instrumental "Spit Me Outta the Whale" is a showcase for Phelps' behind-the-slide playing. **Example 5** begins with a series of hammer-ons played above an alternating-bass pattern. In the third bar, move to a C chord by placing your slide across fret 5. To access the third-fret F, lift the slide slightly away from string 1 and fret the F with your first finger. (Note: Phelps wears his slide on his fourth finger, which frees up his other fingers to fret notes behind the slide.)

Example 6 takes this idea one step further. Begin the figure with your slide across the top three strings at fret 5 and then slide up to fret 7. To nail the descending chromatic lines, from A to Ab to G in bar 1 and from F# to F♮ to E in bar 2, keep the slide in place and lift it slightly while you play the sixth- and fifth-fret notes with

your second and first fingers, respectively. This is a tricky maneuver, so you'll need to be patient in order to pull it off.

For the descending double-stop phrase in **Example 7**, remember to keep your slide low, just covering the strings you're playing with the other fingers of your fretting hand behind the slide. In bar 3, your first and second fingers should be in the perfect place to fret the double-stops on strings 2 and 3.

In "Talking to Jehovah," the benchmark for **Example 8**, Phelps puts his own spin on the classic "Walking Blues" riff popularized by Delta blues players like Robert Johnson and Son House. Instead of a straight alternating bass line, he plays a slightly syncopated bass. Think of the F on string 6, fret 3, as falling into the G note played on the open string.

Example 5

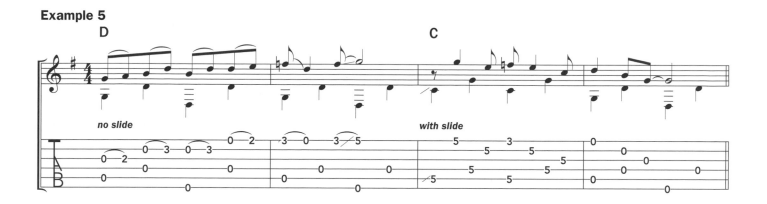

Example 6

Example 7

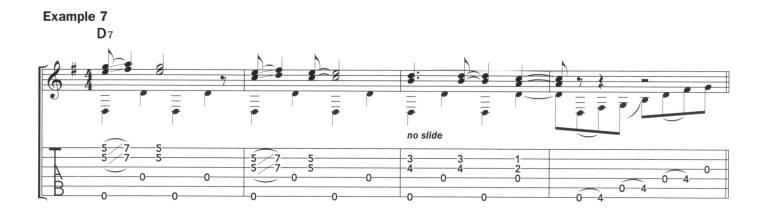

Example 8

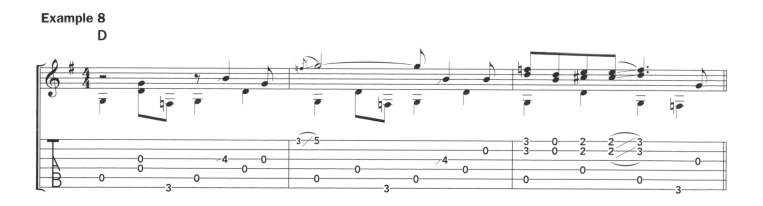

"THE BLUE WHALE"

I've pieced together some of Phelps' open-G ideas in a miniature I call "The Blue Whale" (**Example 9**)—a 14-bar I–IV–V blues in the key of G major. Start out on the I chord (G) with the slide covering strings 1–4 at fret 12. The phrases here wrap around an alternating bass with slide-based melody and a few notes played behind the slide. The slide covers four strings, which might sound a little odd as the fourth-string bass lands at the 12th fret. You could cover only three strings with the slide and use the open strings for the bass, but I find that makes behind-the-slide notes a little more difficult to play.

In bar 5, play the V chord (D) with the slide still covering four strings and just one note, the fifth-fret G on string 1, played behind the slide. It's back to the I chord in bar 7, where you'll do a little descent, from D to C to B, with the slide on string 1.

In the ninth measure, you'll need to move your slide over one string to cover five strings for the C chord. Measures 11–12 use a descending phrase over the V chord, similar to Ex. 7, and the last phrase uses two double pull-offs and a hammer-on in resolving to the I chord. For the double pull-offs make sure to place both your first and second fingers down at the same time.

Once you've mastered "The Blue Whale," try assimilating some of these ideas and techniques—especially the behind-the-slide stuff—in your own bottleneck work. You'll be a deeper player for it.

Example 9
  "The Blue Whale"

Alvin Youngblood Hart

A look inside the style and open tunings of this contemporary bluesman

On one hand, *Big Mama's Door* (Okeh/Sony)—Alvin Youngblood Hart's critically acclaimed 1996 debut album—is like a haunted relic of prewar blues with its covers of Charley Patton ("Pony Blues") and Lead Belly ("The Gallis Pole"). But on the other hand, originals like "Joe Friday," referencing the 1960s television series *Dragnet*, snap us forward in time.

Hart takes a similarly varied approach on his other albums as a leader, from *Territory* (1998) to *Motivational Speaker* (2005), his last solo album. (He continues to tour solo and has recorded on a variety of side projects.) He splits his time between acoustic blues and classic-rock-inspired formats, which can leave some folks scratching their heads. But make no mistake: He always plays the blues like he owns it.

Like a lot of guitarists in the 1960s and '70s, Hart—who spent his formative years in Oakland, California—first discovered music through such rock, pop, and R&B bands as Humble Pie, Thin Lizzy, and the Jackson 5. (Hart even went on to tour with former Thin Lizzy guitarist Gary Moore.) He was also exposed to early blues by his parents—and especially by his grandparents when he visited them in Mississippi. And he spent time in Chicago, playing with some of the elders of the blues scene and earning the name "Youngblood."

IRRESISTIBLE GROOVES IN OPEN G

In his acoustic playing, Hart mines the sonic territory of such blues players as Patton, Robert Johnson, Skip James, and others. He uses open-G (or open-A) and open-D tunings, often in conjunction with a capo, to put his own stamp on the music. He plays finger-style without a pick, on Fraulini and National six-string guitars, as well as various 12-strings, and he leans heavily on single-chord grooves with monotonic bass patterns, in which his picking hand's thumb thumps out a constant four-beat rhythm.

Let's start out with a few exercises that will get you acclimated to playing monotonic grooves. For the first set of exercises, you'll be in open-G (low to high: D G D G B D), with everything falling over the I chord (G7). Later, you'll switch to open-D.

In **Example 1**, play a simple monotonic bass in quarter notes on the open fifth string (G). Keep the bass going in **Example 2** as you add a double stop on beat 1 and the "and" of 3. For the proper groove, be sure to use a metronome. In **Example 3**, there's a more syncopated groove with an eighth-note triplet and a hammer-on. Play the hammer-on with your second and third fingers, and the third-fret notes with your first finger.

Hart tends to limit himself to the first five frets to create irresistible grooves. **Example 4** is similar to what he plays in the instrumental Amazed 'N' Amused" from *Big Mama's Door*. You can play this riff with just one finger—your first—on all the fretted notes. Also inspired by "Amazed 'N' Amused," **Example 5** is similar to a move that Robert Johnson would make in this tuning. Interestingly enough, it can function either as an extension of the I chord or reflect a IV chord change. In this example it's more like an extension of the I chord.

Example 6 is a nod to the opening of "Big Mama's Door" and has a sort of choppy sound. To get that sound, emphasize beats 1 and 3 by plucking the strings with a combination of your index, middle, and ring fingers. Then use your thumb to play the notes on beats 2 and 4 with percussive downstrokes.

Tuning: D G D G B D
(Examples 1–6)

Example 1   Example 2   Example 3

Example 4

Example 5

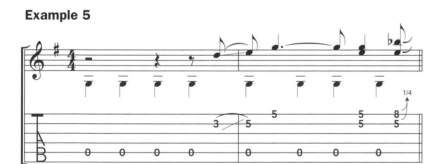

Example 6

OPEN-D MAGIC

Now let's explore Hart's work in open-D tuning, in a series of exercises in the key of D major. The guitarist plays monotonic bass on "If Blues Was Money," which has a riff similar to **Example 7**. Against the bass line, play a descending minor run on the first string that resolves over the second, third, and fourth strings. This kind of groove, even though it's in a major tuning, is reminiscent of such celebrated Skip James songs as "Devil Got My Woman" and "Hard Time Killing Floor Blues," in D- or E-minor tunings.

Example 8 is patterned after what Hart plays over the IV chord (G) in "If Blues Was Money." In the first measure, use a heavy palm mute—rest the side of your picking hand's palm on the strings as you brush the G chord with your thumb. In the second measure, fret the first-string F with your third or fourth finger and give just a slight upward push to produce a quarter-step bend.

SLIDE ON IN

Now it's time to break out the slide. Hart favors a glass bottleneck on his fourth finger, but you can use any type of slide to play **Example 9**, which is informed by the intro and turnaround from "Joe Friday." Start off with a descending run on the second string and play a quick tritone (F♯ and C, implying a D7 chord) before sliding into the double stop on the V chord (A).

Example 10 is similar to the verse of "Joe Friday." It echoes the descending line from the turn-around before it veers up the neck for a slide phrase that descends from the fifth (A) to the third (F♯) to the flatted seventh (C). Hold your slide low—towards the ground—to produce the notes on the first string.

Tuning: D A D F♯ A D
(Examples 7–11)

Example 7

Example 8   Example 9

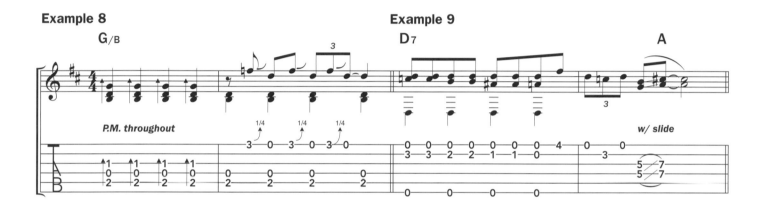

Example 10

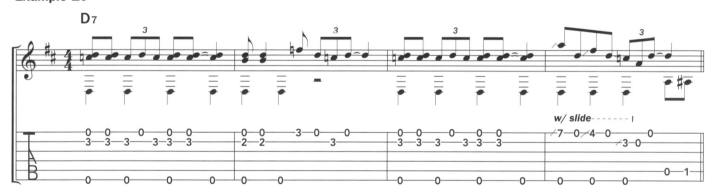

Hart's open-D ideas are put together in **Example 11**, which I'll call "Dragnet Blues." The first five bars borrow the descending line from "Joe Friday," but extend it down the second string and punctuate it with a double stop. Play this five-bar lick twice, on the second pass with a walk up to the IV chord.

The IV-chord (G7) phrase is typical of "Joe Friday" and "If Blues Was Money." Revisit the double-stop lick for the I chord, but in the second bar, play some triplets for more emphasis. Hart doesn't usually play the V chord, but I threw in a line borrowed from Blind Blake's "Police Dog Blues." The phrase gets away from the monotonic bass with a more syncopated lick typical of Blind Blake. The last three measures take you through the IV, I, and V chords, respectively.

Have a listen to *Big Mama's Door* and *Down in the Alley*—Hart's all-acoustic albums—to get a feel and ear for his music. A lot of what he plays is based on prewar blues, but he also mines hillbilly tunes, country, rock, and just about anything else that inspires him. You'll notice he doesn't restrict himself to the 12-bar form; his music is very open- ended. As you put your effort to learning these songs, just remember: Capturing the feel and learning some of the licks is much more important than playing everything note-for-note.

Example 11
"Dragnet Blues"

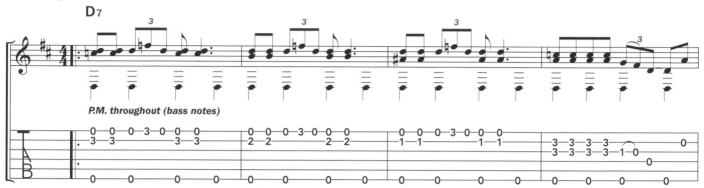

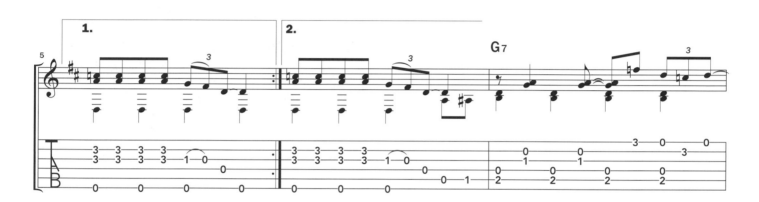

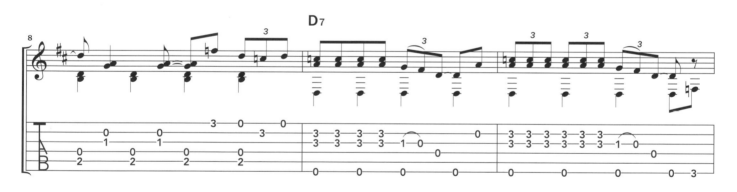

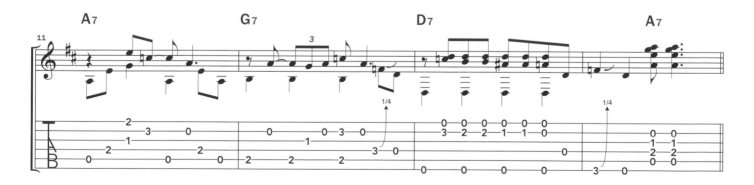

About the Author

Pete Madsen is a San Francisco Bay Area–based acoustic blues, ragtime, and slide guitarist who blends these sounds in his trademark style. He has released three CDs of acoustic music, including his most recent, *Rooster Eggs*, an all-instrumental collection of mostly original material.

Madsen is a longtime guitar instructor and has taught private students, group classes, and workshops throughout California. He has written several instructional books, including *Slide Guitar: Know the Players, Play the Music; Funk Guitar and Bass;* and *The CAGED System for Guitar,* all under the Hal Leonard imprint.

At his regular gigs, Madsen plays songs of the greats—Robert Johnson, Big Bill Broonzy, Blind Blake, John Fahey, and others—as well as original tunes inspired by traditional blues and fingerstyle guitar. His multimedia show, *From the Delta and Beyond*, combines song performances with a slideshow and a brief history of Delta and Piedmont blues.

For more about Madsen, see petemadsenguitar.com.

Essential Listening

Charley Patton
The Complete Recordings: 1929–34 (JSP, 2002)

Elizabeth Cotten
Folksongs and Instrumentals with Guitar (Smithsonian Folkways, 1958)

Memphis Minnie
Crazy Crying Blues (Fabulous, 2002)

Son House
The Legendary Son House: Father of the Folk Blues (Edsel, 1965)
Martin Scorsese Presents the Blues: Son House (Columbia/Sony, 2003)

Skip James
Skip James Today! (Vanguard, 1965)
Devil Got My Woman (Vanguard, 1968)

Tampa Red
It Hurts Me Too: The Essential Recordings of Tampa Red (Indigo, 1994)

Booker White
The Complete Bukka White 1937–1940 (Columbia, 1994)

Robert Johnson
King of the Delta Blues: The Complete Recordings (Columbia/Legacy, 1997)

R. L. Burnside
First Recordings (Fat Possum, 2003)

Jimmy Page
Led Zeppelin (box set compilation) (Atlantic, 1990)

Kelly Joe Phelps
Shine Eyed Mister Zen (Rykodisc, 1999)
Brother Sinner and the Whale (Black Hen Music, 2012)

Alvin Youngblood Hart
Big Mama's Door (Okeh/Sony, 1996)
Down in the Alley (Memphis International, 2002)

PLAY THE BLUES LIKE...

This is one in a series of *Acoustic Guitar Guides* that help you become a better guitarist, a smarter shopper, and a more informed owner and user of guitars and gear.

See the complete collection at **Store.AcousticGuitar.com**.
You'll also find . . .

Magazine

Get to know the music, musicians, and instruments that matter. Monthly magazine for beginning to professional guitarists, teachers, and members of the trade, too.

Books & Downloads

Information, instruction, and inspiration for every guitar player. Reference, how-to, songbooks, and more.

Store

From video lessons, songs, and how-tos to tuners, tees, and tones, the Acoustic Guitar store has something for you.
Visit **store.AcousticGuitar.com** today.

Website

The Acoustic Guitar website features stories you won't want to miss—gear reviews, breaking news, performance videos, giveaways, lessons, and more. Visit **AcousticGuitar.com**.